CW00879783

TRAIN SONGS

TRAIN SONGS

chosen and introduced by

Sean O'Brien

and

Don Paterson

faber and faber

First published in 2013
by Faber and Faber Ltd
Bloomsbury House
74–77 Great Russell Street
London WC1B 3DA

Typeset by RefineCatch Ltd
Printed and bound by CPI Group (UK) Ltd, Croydon, CR0 4YY

A CIP record for this book
is available from the British Library

ISBN 978-0-571-21776-2

FSC
www.fsc.org
MIX
Paper from
responsible sources
FSC® C101712

2 4 6 8 10 9 7 5 3 1

CONTENTS

Introduction ix

PROSPECTS

SEAMUS HEANEY The Railway Children 3
EMILY DICKINSON 'I like to see it lap the Miles' 4
WILLIAM BARNES The Railroad 5
WILLIAM CARLOS WILLIAMS Overture to a Dance
  of Locomotives 6
WALT WHITMAN To a Locomotive in Winter 8
ROBERT LOUIS STEVENSON From a Railway Carriage 10
ELIZABETH BISHOP Chemin de Fer 11
KENNETH KOCH One Train May Hide Another 12
LES MURRAY The Away-bound Train 15
RUTH STONE Train Ride 18
FRANCES CORNFORD To a Fat Lady Seen from a Train 19
WILLIAM STAFFORD Vacation 20
RANDALL JARRELL The Orient Express 21
STEPHEN SPENDER The Express 23
PETER DIDSBURY The Guitar 24
ANON Working on the Railroad 26
CHARLES SIMIC Leaving an Unknown City 28
PAUL FARLEY From a Weekend First 29
JAMES WRIGHT A Poem Written under an Archway in a
  Discontinued Railroad Station in Fargo, North Dakota 31
HUGO WILLIAMS Now That I Hear Trains 32
NORMAN DUBIE The Train 33
PHILIP LARKIN The Whitsun Weddings 35
FLANDERS AND SWANN The Slow Train 38

[v]

MARK WALDRON The Very Slow Train 40
ALAN BROWNJOHN The Train 41
WILLIAM WORDSWORTH On the Projected Kendal and
    Windermere Railway 42

STATIONS

WALTER DE LA MARE The Railway Junction 45
SIMON ARMITAGE The Metaphor Now Standing at Platform 8 47
W. H. AUDEN Gare du Midi 49
EDWARD THOMAS Adlestrop 50
JOHN BETJEMAN Pershore Station, *or* A Liverish Journey
    First Class 51
WILFRED OWEN The Send-Off 52
FRANCES CORNFORD Parting in Wartime 53
THOM GUNN Berlin in Ruins 54
PATRICK MCGUINNESS Correspondances 56
CHRISTOPHER MIDDLETON Pointed Boots 57
JOHN MONTAGUE All Legendary Obstacles 58
DENNIS O'DRISCOLL A Station 59
LOUIS SIMPSON The Unwritten Poem 61
U. A. FANTHORPE Father in the Railway Buffet 62
IAN HAMILTON Pretending Not to Sleep 63
TONY HARRISON Changing at York 64
MICHAEL HOFMANN Nighthawks 65
HELEN DUNMORE The marshalling yard 67
PHILIP LARKIN Friday Night in the Royal Station Hotel 69
DANNIE ABSE Not Adlestrop 70
WISLAWA SZYMBORSKA The Railroad Station 71

UNDERGROUND

EZRA POUND In a Station of the Metro 75
MICHAEL DONAGHY Poem On The Underground 76

SEAMUS HEANEY District and Circle 78
SEAMUS HEANEY The Underground 81
W. N. HERBERT Comrade Bear 82
EDWIN MORGAN The Piranhas 83
MATTHEW SWEENEY Tube Ride to Martha's 84
CHARLES REZNIKOFF *from* Jerusalem the Golden 85

TRAVELLERS

ROBERT JOHNSON Love in Vain Blues 91
WENDY COPE 'Indeed, 'tis true' 92
HUGO WILLIAMS Day Return 93
SHERMAN ALEXIE On The Amtrak From Boston To
    New York City 94
JOHN ASHBERY Melodic Trains 96
JOHN BETJEMAN Thoughts in a Train 99
JOHN FULLER In a Railway Compartment 100
ELMA MITCHELL The Passenger Opposite 101
DOUGLAS DUNN Renfrewshire Traveller 103
PAUL DURCAN Tullynoe: Tête-à-Tête in the Parish
    Priest's Parlour 105
LOUIS MACNEICE Corner Seat 107
DAN PAGIS Written in Pencil in the Sealed Freight Car 108
LES MURRAY Troop Train Returning 109
PETER PORTER On the Train Between Wellington and
    Shrewsbury 111
JEAN SPRACKLAND The Stopped Train 114
HUGO WILLIAMS Toilet 116
RUTH STONE 'The widow likes to ride on trains' 118
ROBERT CRAWFORD The Railway Library 119
IAN DUHIG Jericho Shandy 121
THOMAS MCCARTHY The Emigration Trains 125
MICHAEL LONGLEY Couchette 127

NORMAN MACCAIG Sleeping Compartment 128
LOUISE GLÜCK The Chicago Train 129
LOUIS MACNEICE Figure of Eight 130
CIARAN CARSON Yes 131
GRETE TARTLER Orient Express 132
CAROL ANN DUFFY The Way My Mother Speaks 133

NIGHT

ANON The Midnight Special 137
T. S. ELIOT Skimbleshanks: the Railway Cat 139
W. H. AUDEN Night Mail 142
THOMAS HARDY The Missed Train 145
WILLIAM MCGONAGALL The Tay Bridge Disaster 146
EDNA ST VINCENT MILLAY Travel 149
PAUL MULDOON The Train 150
SAM PHILLIPS AND JUNIOR PARKER Mystery Train 151
LINDA PASTAN At the Train Museum 153
CARL SANDBURG Limited 154
DAVE SMITH Cumberland Station 155
KEN SMITH Zoo Station midnight 158
JAMES THOMSON In the Train 159
KATRINA PORTEOUS If My Train Will Come 160
GEORGE SZIRTES Ghost Train 161
TOM WAITS Train Song 163
LOUIS MACNEICE Charon 164
NORMAN NICHOLSON Coastal Journey 165

Acknowledgements 167

Index of Poets 171

INTRODUCTION

Readers will not be surprised to learn that there is no shortage of poems about trains and railways. The age of steam in particular lends itself as readily to poetry as do love, death and the natural world, because the railway train participates in all of them. It is hard to name an invention since the Industrial Revolution which has proved as accommodating to poetry as the train, while among its predecessors perhaps only the book and the ship have offered so much to the imagination. In comparison the car seems poetically negligible (though rock and roll has done it honour) while space travel is as yet an extremely rare alternative to cocaine for those who have too much money.

So it would not be difficult to assemble a railway anthology along what seem like familiar lines, stoked by nostalgia and comfortably uncoupled from the insistent realities of politics, economics and war. That is not what we wanted to do, and the experience of preparing this book has taught us afresh that the train's songs are not only many but ungovernably various and yet mysteriously connected. Ken Smith's Zoo Station at midnight is not much like Edward Thomas's Adlestrop, which does not resemble Auden's Gare du Midi, yet all are accessible to each other by train. Despite her rather different concerns Ruth Stone's 'Train Ride' might pass Elvis Presley's mysterious long black train en route. Jean Sprackland and Hugo Williams might be seated on the same stopped train, entertaining their very different thoughts. Flanders and Swann's sweet elegy for the death of the slow train at the hands of Dr Beeching seems hardly to be part of the same universe as Dan Pagis's desperate note from a train bound for the Nazi death camps, though clearly it is.

It would take another Bradshaw and unlimited resources to devise a schedule for the multitude of journeys poets have taken. We have instead favoured a vivid sample based on our own enthusiasms but at times hospitable to poems that, rightly or wrongly, passengers expect to find along the permanent way.

Part of the train's appeal is its relationship to time. The train moves into the future on its iron road while provoking a complex nostalgia that has accompanied it since birth. Almost as soon as the railway arrived in Britain it began to depart. After the railway boom of the 1840s, the empire of the tracks seems always to have been defending and withdrawing from its own frontiers, even as the railways underwent growth on a continental scale in Europe and the Americas.

In the USA the history of the railroad has proved more ruthless: the train created the modern nation in its drive westward, and entered the poetic imagination indelibly as it did so, in blues and workmen's songs, but America now often seems for the most part a land of torn-up tracks and demolished bridges where the lonesome whistle must be heard in memory rather than fact. John Fogerty's cross-tie walker, navigating his discontents along the tracks, would find he had nowhere to go.

Got no sand in my pocket, you know I ain't tied down.
Ain't no sand in my pocket, never do sit down.
I'm just a cross-tie walker, where the freight trains run.
Run, run, run, run.

If you see me acomin', don't you waste my time.
If you see me acomin', don't you waste my time.
'Cause there's more miles between us than the Santa Fe Line.
Run, run, run, run.

The very experience of train travel seems unknown to many US citizens nowadays and, like the bus, the train is often associated with poverty, at a time when in Britain the cost of taking the train is becoming a luxury rather than a matter of everyday utility. Our societies have often used the train badly, yet we know it to be as close as earthly things come to perfection.

The train is a time machine that works in both directions and in none. Time can be made to stop when the train moves us to reverie. Lost time can also be fleetingly regained by travellers in restored carriages on lines preserved by the generous monomania of enthusiasts, even as the engine with its scarves of smoke and steam moves away into the future. As Douglas Dunn wrote in 'Going to Bed', 'sonorous locomotives pull away from time / into the night of may-blossom'. It is no accident that the most famous illustration of relativity involves an observer in one train watching another train pass.

Such a vehicle of mystery and paradox could have been purpose-built for the poet. It is unfortunate that outside the sphere of steampunk we shall never know what Donne and Marvell would have made of the engine, the parallel tracks, the irresistible forces and immoveable objects. On the other hand, we certainly do know what Wordsworth thought when a railway to Windermere was proposed: he was by no means keen. This was the Wordsworth who wrote sonnets in favour of capital punishment, rather than the one who knew the experience of bliss.

Since his time, though, the notion of the rural has for many become inextricably bound up with the railway. The arrival of a train at a country halt, as in 'Adlestrop', seems the very definition of Georgian pastoral in the early twentieth century. And at the same time a largely townee population has used the view from the carriage window as evidence of another, preferable England where things are done differently and better, in the colours of any preferred decade – at which point the borders of imagination and sentimentality threaten to blur, and the view needs the refreshment of a more problematic response. One such is Lars von Trier's deranged cine-poem, *Europa*, which opens with tracks disappearing into the dark behind a train, while Max von Sydow intones: 'You are now entering

Europa', namely Germany, to which an idealistic young exile has returned just after the war to work as a sleeping-car attendant as the rail system is rebuilt amid the ruins of the defeated nation, while stay-behind Nazi Werwolf units sabotage the trains in the permanent night of the film. The industrialized railway-driven nightmare of the Holocaust is evoked the more starkly by remaining unseen. If it were possible to transform *Europa* into language we would have included it here.

In the popular imagination, though, where trains go romance follows. The train was made for the cinema as well as for poets. Hitchcock understood the eroticism of the time capsule of the railway carriage: his heroes and heroines meet on trains in England (*The Thirty-Nine Steps*), the Balkans (*The Lady Vanishes*) and in the American Midwest (*North by Northwest*). In this view life is dangerous, glamorous and exciting, with a strong narrative shape. The traveller in Britain, at any rate, knows this not to be true, but lives in hope of a suspension of ordinariness. As for ordinariness, in one of the best of all railway poems Philip Larkin presents a time – the mid-1950s – when couples would set out by rail for their honeymoons (and when Whitsun was still a significant date in the calendar). There's not much glamour in 'The Whitsun Weddings' – it is a study of provincial England – but there is a sense of quiet awe at human possibility in the closing image of the arrow-shower fired 'as the tightened brakes took hold'.

The railway is also a place of work – the hard, brutal work of the Irish navvies who built Britain's railway system, and of the railroad gangs whose labours gave America a new geography, and of the East Kentucky miners who dug coal to drive the trains and used the trains to escape into town to drink and chase women and fend off the inevitable in Merle Travis's 'Nine Pound Hammer':

> Well it's a long way to Harlan,
> It's a long way to Hazard,

Just to get a little brew,
Just to get a little brew.
When I'm long gone,
You can make my tombstone,
Outta number nine coal,
Outta number nine coal.

In closing, let us turn to eloquence of a different kind, from the late Tony Judt, who sums up the meaning and value of railways with a clarity that brooks no argument:

If we lose the railways we shall not just have lost a valuable practical asset whose replacement or recovery would be intolerably expensive. We shall have acknowledged that we have forgotten how to live collectively. If we throw away the railway stations and the lines leading to them – as we began to do in the 1950s and 1960s – we shall be throwing away our memory of how to live the confident civic life. It is not by chance that Margaret Thatcher – who famously declared that 'there is no such thing as Society. There are individual men and women, and there are families' – made a point of never travelling by train. If we cannot spend our collective resources on trains and travel contentedly in them it is not because we have joined gated communities and need nothing but private cars to move between them. It will be because we have become gated *individuals* who don't know how to share public space to common advantage. The implications of such a loss would far transcend the demise of one system of transport among others. It would mean we had done with modern life.

Amen to that.

PROSPECTS

SEAMUS HEANEY

The Railway Children

When we climbed the slopes of the cutting
We were eye-level with the white cups
Of the telegraph poles and the sizzling wires.

Like lovely freehand they curved for miles
East and miles west beyond us, sagging
Under their burden of swallows.

We were small and thought we knew nothing
Worth knowing. We thought words travelled the wires
In the shiny pouches of raindrops,

Each one seeded full with the light
Of the sky, the gleam of the lines, and ourselves
So infinitesimally scaled

We could stream through the eye of a needle.

'I like to see it lap the Miles'

I like to see it lap the Miles –
And lick the Valleys up –
And stop to feed itself at Tanks –
And then – prodigious step

Around a Pile of Mountains –
And supercilious peer
In Shanties – by the sides of Roads –
And then a Quarry pare

To fit its Ribs
And crawl between
Complaining all the while
In horrid – hooting stanza –
Then chase itself down Hill –

And neigh like Boanerges –
Then – punctual as a Star
Stop – docile and omnipotent
At its own stable door –

WILLIAM BARNES

The Railroad

I took a flight, awhile agoo,
Along the raïls, a stage or two,
An' while the heavy wheels did spin
An' rottle, wi' a deafnèn din,
In clouds o' steam, the zweepèn traïn
Did shoot along the hill-bound plaïn,
As sheädes o' birds in flight, do pass
Below em on the zunny grass.
An' as I zot, an' look'd abrade
On leänen land an' windèn road,

The ground a-spread along our flight
Did vlee behind us out o' zight;
The while the zun, our heav'nly guide,
Did ride on wi' us, zide by zide.
An' zoo, while time, vrom stage to stage,
Do car us on vrom youth to age,
The e'thly pleasures we do vind
Be soon a-met, an' left behind;
But God, beholdèn vrom above
Our lowly road, wi' yearnèn love,
Do keep bezide us, stage by stage,
Vrom be'th to youth, vrom youth to age.

WILLIAM CARLOS WILLIAMS

Overture to a Dance of Locomotives

Men with picked voices chant the names
of cities in a huge gallery: promises
that pull through descending stairways
to a deep rumbling.

The rubbing feet
of those coming to be carried quicken a
grey pavement into soft light that rocks
to and fro, under the domed ceiling,
across and across from pale
earthcolored walls of bare limestone.

Covertly the hands of a great clock
go round and round! Were they to
move quickly and at once the whole
secret would be out and the shuffling
of all ants be done forever.

A leaning pyramid of sunlight, narrowing
out at a high window, moves by the clock:
disaccordant hands straining out from
a center: inevitable postures infinitely
repeated –
two – twofour – twoeight!
Porters in red hats run on narrow platforms.
This way ma'am!

– important not to take
the wrong train!
Lights from the concrete
ceiling hang crooked but –
Poised horizontal
on glittering parallels the dingy cylinders
packed with a warm glow – inviting entry –
pull against the hour. But brakes can
hold a fixed posture till –
The whistle!

Not twoeight. Not twofour. Two!

Gliding windows. Colored cooks sweating
in a small kitchen. Taillights –

In time: twofour!
In time: twoeight!

– rivers are tunneled: trestles
cross oozy swampland: wheels repeating
the same gesture remain relatively
stationary: rails forever parallel
return on themselves infinitely.
The dance is sure.

WALT WHITMAN

To a Locomotive in Winter

Thee for my recitative,
Thee in the driving storm even as now, the snow, the
    winter-day declining,
Thee in thy panoply, thy measur'd dual throbbing and thy beat
    convulsive,
Thy black cylindric body, golden brass and silvery steel,
Thy ponderous side-bars, parallel and connecting rods, gyrating,
    shuttling at thy sides,
Thy metrical, now swelling pant and roar, now tapering in the
    distance,
Thy great protruding head-light fix'd in front,
Thy long, pale, floating vapor-pennants, tinged with delicate
    purple,
The dense and murky clouds out-belching from thy smoke-stack,
Thy knitted frame, thy springs and valves, the tremulous twinkle
    of thy wheels,
Thy train of cars behind, obedient, merrily following,
Through gale or calm, now swift, now slack, yet steadily
    careering;
Type of the modern – emblem of motion and power – pulse of the
    continent,
For once come serve the Muse and merge in verse, even as here I
    see thee,
With storm and buffeting gusts of wind and falling snow,
By day thy warning ringing bell to sound its notes,
By night thy silent signal lamps to swing.

Fierce-throated beauty!
Roll through my chant with all thy lawless music, thy swinging
    lamps at night,
Thy madly-whistled laughter, echoing, rumbling like an
    earthquake, rousing all,
Law of thyself complete, thine own track firmly holding,
(No sweetness debonair of tearful harp or glib piano thine,)
Thy trills of shrieks by rocks and hills return'd,
Launch'd o'er the prairies wide, across the lakes,
To the free skies unpent and glad and strong.

From a Railway Carriage

Faster than fairies, faster than witches,
Bridges and houses, hedges and ditches;
And charging along like troops in a battle,
All through the meadows the horses and cattle:
All of the sights of the hill and the plain
Fly as thick as driving rain;
And ever again, in the wink of an eye,
Painted stations whistle by.

Here is a child who clambers and scrambles,
All by himself and gathering brambles;
Here is a tramp who stands and gazes;
And there is the green for stringing the daisies!
Here is a cart run away in the road
Lumping along with man and load;
And here is a mill and there is a river:
Each a glimpse and gone for ever!

Chemin de Fer

Alone on the railroad track
    I walked with pounding heart.
The ties were too close together
    or maybe too far apart.

The scenery was impoverished:
    scrub-pine and oak; beyond
its mingled gray-green foliage
    I saw the little pond

where the dirty hermit lives,
    lie like an old tear
holding onto its injuries
    lucidly year after year.

The hermit shot off his shot-gun
    and the tree by his cabin shook.
Over the pond went a ripple.
    The pet hen went chook-chook.

'Love should be put into action!'
    screamed the old hermit.
Across the pond an echo
    tried and tried to confirm it.

One Train May Hide Another

(sign at a railroad crossing in Kenya)

In a poem, one line may hide another line,
As at a crossing, one train may hide another train.
That is, if you are waiting to cross
The tracks, wait to do it for one moment at
Least after the first train is gone. And so when you read
Wait until you have read the next line –
Then it is safe to go on reading.
In a family one sister may conceal another,
So, when you are courting, it's best to have them all in view
Otherwise in coming to find one you may love another.
One father or one brother may hide the man,
If you are a woman, whom you have been waiting to love.
So always standing in front of something the other
As words stand in front of objects, feelings, and ideas.
One wish may hide another. And one person's reputation may hide
The reputation of another. One dog may conceal another
On a lawn, so if you escape the first one you're not necessarily safe;
One lilac may hide another and then a lot of lilacs and on the
    Appia Antica one tomb
May hide a number of other tombs. In love, one reproach may
    hide another,
One small complaint may hide a great one.
One injustice may hide another – one colonial may hide another,
One blaring red uniform another, and another, a whole column.
    One bath may hide another bath
As when, after bathing, one walks out into the rain.

One idea may hide another: Life is simple
Hide Life is incredibly complex, as in the prose of Gertrude Stein
One sentence hides another and is another as well. And in the
    laboratory
One invention may hide another invention,
One evening may hide another, one shadow, a nest of shadows.
One dark red, or one blue, or one purple – this is a painting
By someone after Matisse. One waits at the tracks until they pass,
These hidden doubles or, sometimes, likenesses. One identical twin
May hide the other. And there may be even more in there! The
    obstetrician
Gazes at the Valley of the Var. We used to live there, my wife and
    I, but
One life hid another life. And now she is gone and I am here.
A vivacious mother hides a gawky daughter. The daughter hides
Her own vivacious daughter in turn. They are in
A railway station and the daughter is holding a bag
Bigger than her mother's bag and successfully hides it.
In offering in pick up the daughter's bag one finds oneself
    confronted by the mother's
And has to carry that one, too. So one hitchhiker
May deliberately hide another and one cup of coffee
Another, too, until one is over-excited. One love may hide another
    love or the same love
As when 'I love you' suddenly rings false and one discovers
The better love lingering behind, as when 'I'm full of doubts'
Hides 'I'm certain about something and it is that'
And one dream may hide another as is well known, always, too. In
    the Garden of Eden
Adam and Eve may hide the real Adam and Eve.
Jerusalem may hide another Jerusalem.
When you come to something, stop to let it pass
So you can see what else is there. At home, no matter where,

Internal tracks pose dangers, too: one memory
Certainly hides another, that being what memory is all about,
The eternal reverse succession of contemplated entities. Reading
    A Sentimental Journey look around
When you have finished, for *Tristram Shandy*, to see
If it is standing there, it should be, stronger
And more profound and theretofore hidden as Santa Maria
    Maggiore
May be hidden by similar churches inside Rome. One sidewalk
May hide another, as when you're asleep there, and
One song hide another song; a pounding upstairs
Hide the beating of drums. One friend may hide another, you sit
    at the foot of a tree
With one and when you get up to leave there is another
Whom you'd have preferred to talk to all along. One teacher,
One doctor, one ecstasy, one illness, one woman, one man
May hide another. Pause to let the first one pass.
You think, Now it is safe to cross and you are hit by the next one.
    It can be important
To have waited at least a moment to see what was already there.

The Away-bound Train

for Con Kiriloff

I stand in a house of trees, and it is evening:
at the foot of the stairs, a creek runs grey with sand.

A rocking, unending dim sound,
a racket as if of a train,
wears through my sleep, and I wake
to find it late afternoon

at which I sit up, rub my eyes –
beneath us, the carriage-wheels moan
on their winter-wet, wind-polished rails,
but the train hurries on, hurries on.

The loco horn beams out its admonition
at a weatherboard village standing on the fields.

The near hills rise steeply and fall,
the hills farther off settle down:
I light up a cigarette, wipe
my breath from the cold window-pane.

The upland farms are all bare,
except where dark, storm-matted fern
has found its way down from the heights,
or landslides have brought down raw stone

for, outside, it's silent July,
when wet rocks stare from the hills
and thistles grow, and the rain
walks with the wind through the fields –

and this is my country, passing by me forever:
beyond these hills and paddocks lies the world.

Outside, it is timeless July,
when horses' hoofs puncture the chill
green ground, mud dogging their steps,
and summer's plough sleeps in the barn,

when rabbits camp up in the mouths
of flooded burrows, and dogs
under creekbanks wince at the thump
of a gun fired close to the earth.

The cold time, the season of clouds
beyond the end of the year,
when boxwood chunks glare in the stove –
but that is the past. I am here.

I look across the clear, receding landscape:
from a distant ridge, a horseman eyes the train.

The train never slackens its speed:
an iron bridge echoes, is gone,
on the far bank, twilit and tall,
the green timber gathers us in.

And we dash through the forest, my face,
reflected, wanders and sways

on the glass of the windowpane, and
I press my nose to my nose . . .

the loco horn sounds far across the uplands:
a man with no past has all too many futures.

I take out a book, read a phrase
five times – and put the book down.
The window-sash chatters. My mind
trails far in the wake of the train

where, away in the left-behind hills,
through paddock and cattlecamp I
go drifting down valleys towards
the peopled country of sleep . . .

I wait in the house. It is raining in the forest.
If I move or speak, the house will not be there.

RUTH STONE

Train Ride

All things come to an end;
small calves in Arkansas,
the bend of the muddy river.
Do all things come to an end?
No, they go on forever.
They go on forever, the swamp,
the vine-choked cypress, the oaks
rattling last year's leaves,
the thump of the rails, the kite,
the still white stilted heron.
All things come to an end.
The red clay bank, the spread hawk,
the bodies riding this train,
the stalled truck, pale sunlight, the talk;
the talk goes on forever,
the wide dry field of geese,
a man stopped near his porch
to watch. Release, release;
between cold death and a fever,
send what you will, I will listen.
All things come to an end.
No, they go on forever.

FRANCES CORNFORD

To a Fat Lady Seen from a Train

O why do you walk through the fields in gloves,
    Missing so much and so much?
O fat white woman whom nobody loves,
    Why do you walk through the fields in gloves,
When the grass is soft as the breast of doves
    And shivering-sweet to the touch?
O why do you walk through the fields in gloves,
    Missing so much and so much?

WILLIAM STAFFORD

Vacation

One scene as I bow to pour her coffee: –

Three Indians in the scouring drouth
huddle at a grave scooped in the gravel,
lean to the wind as our train goes by.
Someone is gone.
There is dust on everything in Nevada.

I pour the cream.

The Orient Express

One looks from the train
Almost as one looked as a child. In the sunlight
What I see still seems to me plain,
I am safe; but at evening
As the lands darken, a questioning
Precariousness comes over everything.

Once after a day of rain
I lay longing to be cold; and after a while
I was cold again, and hunched shivering
Under the quilt's many colors, gray
With the dull ending of the winter day.
Outside me there were a few shapes
Of chairs and tables, things from a primer;
Outside the window
There were the chairs and tables of the world. . .
I saw that the world
That had seemed to me the plain
Gray mask of all that was strange
Behind it – of all that *was* – was all.

But it is beyond belief.
One thinks, 'Behind everything
An unforced joy, an unwilling
Sadness (a willing sadness, a forced joy)
Moves changelessly'; one looks from the train
And there is something, the same thing

Behind everything: all these little villages,
A passing woman, a field of grain,
The man who says good-bye to his wife –
A path through a wood full of lives, and the train
Passing, after all unchangeable
And not now ever to stop, like a heart –

It is like any other work of art.
It is and never can be changed.
Behind everything there is always
The unknown unwanted life.

STEPHEN SPENDER

The Express

After the first powerful plain manifesto
The black statement of pistons, without more fuss
But gliding like a queen, she leaves the station.
Without bowing and with restrained unconcern
She passes the houses which humbly crowd outside,
The gasworks and at last the heavy page
Of death, printed by gravestones in the cemetery.
Beyond the town there lies the open country
Where, gathering speed, she acquires mystery,
The luminous self-possession of ships on ocean.
It is now she begins to sing – at first quite low
Then loud, and at last with a jazzy madness –
The song of her whistle screaming at curves,
Of deafening tunnels, brakes, innumerable bolts.
And always light, aerial, underneath
Goes the elate metre of her wheels.
Steaming through metal landscape on her lines
She plunges new eras of wild happiness
Where speed throws up strange shapes, broad curves
And parallels clean like the steel of guns.
At last, further than Edinburgh or Rome,
Beyond the crest of the world, she reaches night
Where only a low streamline brightness
Of phosphorus on the tossing hills is white.
Ah, like a comet through flame, she moves entranced
Wrapt in her music no bird song, no, nor bough
Breaking with honey buds, shall ever equal.

[23]

The Guitar

And what if all of animated nature
Be but organic Harps diversely fram'd,
That tremble into thought . . .

COLERIDGE

Aerial songs, estuarial poetry.
An electric guitar is being played.
Its neck is five miles long,
and forms a margin of the River Humber,
where the thin soils are.
Aeolus swoops down, and begins to bounce on it.
He has serpents in his eyes.
He plucks the strings
with his Nebuchadnezzar toenails.
He's composing a piece called Early Memorials.
A train comes. His pinions take him
half a mile high in a lift.
The train courses over
the frets of the guitar,
but it is going backwards,
towards the hole in the middle.
Coleridge is sitting at a window
with his back towards the engine.
He must have been lunching in Goole,
but now he's fallen asleep.
'Dutch River,' he murmurs, 'Dutch River.'
He's dreaming of the advent of the railways
but will not remember, because I intend to

keep it from him.
It's a mercy that is available to me.
The train steams through fields of bright chives,
then it reverses and comes back as a diesel.
A madman steps out of a cabin and salutes it.
He stands by the flagpole outside his summer *kraal.*
The engine-driver waves.
The engine-driver and the madman
both went to the same school as me.
They sport the red blazer and the nose.
They chat for a bit while the engine grazes
on the chives that spring up through the ballast.
'Nice bit of road,' one says. 'Aye, nice road,' says the other.
The sky is like an entry in The Oxford English Dictionary.
The earliest reference for it is 1764,
in Randall's *Semi-Virgilian Husbandry.*
The loco swings its head from side to side
with the movements of an old-fashioned camera,
or a caterpillar. The mythic god of the winds, however,
who is still aloft, is getting tired of attending.
He flies up the line and starts twisting on the pegs.
Lunatic, driver, and diesel all look up.
Their faces assume an almost communal rictus.
They all jump in the carriage with Coleridge,
as the mighty lexicon twangs. They wish they were asleep.
The god puts his face right up to the window
and shakes his horrid locks at them.
They stare at the cattle grazing in his fields.
They note the herbaceous stubble
which makes frightful his visage of mud.

Working on the Railroad

I've been working on the railroad
All the live-long day.
I've been working on the railroad
Just to pass the time away.

Can't you hear the whistle blowing,
Rise up so early in the morn;
Can't you hear the captain shouting,
'Dinah, blow your horn!'

Dinah, won't you blow,
Dinah, won't you blow,
Dinah, won't you blow your horn?
Dinah, won't you blow,
Dinah, won't you blow,
Dinah, won't you blow your horn?

Someone's in the kitchen with Dinah
Someone's in the kitchen I know
Someone's in the kitchen with Dinah
Strummin' on the old *banjo*!

Singin' fee, fie, fiddly-i-o
Fee, fie, fiddly-i-o-o-o-o
Fee, fie, fiddly-i-o
Strummin' on the old banjo.

Someone's makin' love to Dinah
Someone's making love I know.
Someone's making love to Dinah
'Cause I can't hear the old banjo.

Leaving an Unknown City

That mutt with ribs showing
We left standing near a garbage truck
With a most hopeful look,
His tail on the verge of happiness
As the train picked up speed
The outcome left open

With the dusk falling rapidly
Making the dusty windows reflect
Our five traveling companions
Sitting with hat-shrouded eyes,
The absent-minded smiles
Already firmly set on each face.

PAUL FARLEY

From a Weekend First

One for the money. Arrangements in green and grey
from the window of an empty dining-car.
No takers for this Burgundy today
apart from me. I'll raise a weighted stem
to my homeland scattering by, be grateful for
these easy-on-the-eye, Army & Navy
surplus camouflage colours that seem
to mask all trace of life and industry;

a draft for the hidden dead, our forefathers,
the landfills of the mind where they turned in
with the plush and orange peel of yesteryear,
used up and entertained and put to bed
at last; to this view where everything seems to turn
on the middle distance. Crematoria, multiplex
way stations in the form of big sheds
that house their promises of goods and sex;

to the promise of a university town,
its spires and playing fields. No border guards
will board at this station, no shakedown
relieve me of papers or contraband:
this is *England*. Nobody will pull the cord
on these thoughts, though the cutlery and glasses
set for dinner are tinkling at a bend,
a carriage full of ghosts taking their places.

Now drink to slow outskirts, the colour wheels
of fifty years collected in windows;
to worlds of interiors, to credit deals
with nothing to pay until next year, postcodes
where water hardens, then softens, where rows
of streetlights become the dominant motif
as day drains, and I see myself transposed
into the dark, lifting my glass. Belief

is one thing, though the dead have none of it.
What would they make of me? This pinot noir
on my expenses, time enough to write
this on a Virgin antimacassar –
the miles of feint, the months of Sunday school,
the gallons of free milk, all led to here:
an empty dining-car, a single fool
reflected endlessly on the night air.

JAMES WRIGHT

A Poem Written under an Archway in a Discontinued Railroad Station, Fargo, North Dakota

Outside the great clanging cathedrals of rust and smoke,
The locomotives browse on sidings.
They pause, exhausted by the silence of prairies.
Sometimes they leap and cry out, skitterish.
They fear dark little boys in Ohio,
Who know how to giggle without breathing,
Who sneak out of graveyards in summer twilights
And lay crossties across rails.
The rattle of coupling pins still echoes
In the smoke stains,
The Cincinnati of the dead.
Around the bend now, beyond the grain elevators,
The late afternoon limited wails
Savage with the horror and loneliness of a child, lost
And dragged by a glad cop through a Chicago terminal.
The noose tightens, the wail stops, and I am leaving.
Across the street, an arthritic man
Takes coins at the parking lot.
He smiles with the sinister grief
Of old age.

HUGO WILLIAMS

Now That I Hear Trains

Now that I hear trains
whistling out of Paddington on their way to Wales,
I like to think of him, as young as he was then,
running behind me along the sand,
holding my saddle steady
and launching me off on my own.

Now that I look unlike
the boy on the brand new bike
who wobbled away down the beach,
I hear him telling me: 'Keep pedalling, keep pedalling.'
When I looked over my shoulder
he was nowhere to be seen.

NORMAN DUBIE

The Train

Accident could be a god to little boys.

The way they hurt their necks
To look through glass down to the twisted
Wreckage in the gorge. The conductor
Telling the ladies from Jamaica
We are one stop from the border. The older
Of the two is shocked by a sudden pasture
Beside the lake, icehouses
Left there for the summer – she says, 'Oh, Chloe,
Look at the shanties; to think
There is such poverty in Maine.' She begins
To finger the pearls sewn into the shoulder
Of her dress; the diamond she's wearing
Has the fire of fat in it. And then
A tunnel, and then more birches with the lake again.

You smile at me and look across
To the girl in black stockings who is asleep,
Her lips
Moving, her skirt rising with the jumping train.
You straighten your blouse. Sharing
A thermos of coffee, we have said twice
That we'll be late for the station. Beyond the window
The day lilies are a smudged crayon.

Who is drowning in the lake? Whose father
Is falling on the stairs? Which of us
Racing north will be truly late? We are
All annoyed, stepping out into the rain.
The city that we raced for, racing for its own sake.
The girl in black stockings is waking on the corner.

She has ruined the hard parallelism of the rain.
She said her brother died in the jungle last week.
We said, with intonation, what a shame.

The Whitsun Weddings

That Whitsun, I was late getting away:
   Not till about
One-twenty on the sunlit Saturday
Did my three-quarters-empty train pull out,
All windows down, all cushions hot, all sense
Of being in a hurry gone. We ran
Behind the backs of houses, crossed a street
Of blinding windscreens, smelt the fish-dock; thence
The river's level drifting breadth began,
Where sky and Lincolnshire and water meet.

All afternoon, through the tall heat that slept
   For miles inland,
A slow and stopping curve southwards we kept.
Wide farms went by, short-shadowed cattle, and
Canals with floatings of industrial froth;
A hothouse flashed uniquely: hedges dipped
And rose: and now and then a smell of grass
Displaced the reek of buttoned carriage-cloth
Until the next town, new and nondescript,
Approached with acres of dismantled cars.

At first, I didn't notice what a noise
   The weddings made
Each station that we stopped at: sun destroys
The interest of what's happening in the shade,
And down the long cool platforms whoops and skirls

I took for porters larking with the mails,
And went on reading. Once we started, though,
We passed them, grinning and pomaded, girls
In parodies of fashion, heels and veils,
All posed irresolutely, watching us go,

As if out on the end of an event
   Waving goodbye
To something that survived it. Struck, I leant
More promptly out next time, more curiously,
And saw it all again in different terms:
The fathers with broad belts under their suits
And seamy foreheads; mothers loud and fat;
An uncle shouting smut; and then the perms,
The nylon gloves and jewellery-substitutes,
The lemons, mauves, and olive-ochres that

Marked off the girls unreally from the rest.
   Yes, from cafés
And banquet-halls up yards, and bunting-dressed
Coach-party annexes, the wedding-days
Were coming to an end. All down the line
Fresh couples climbed aboard: the rest stood round;
The last confetti and advice were thrown,
And, as we moved, each face seemed to define
Just what it saw departing: children frowned
At something dull; fathers had never known

Success so huge and wholly farcical;
   The women shared
The secret like a happy funeral;
While girls, gripping their handbags tighter, stared
At a religious wounding. Free at last,

And loaded with the sum of all they saw,
We hurried towards London, shuffling gouts of steam.
Now fields were building-plots, and poplars cast
Long shadows over major roads, and for
Some fifty minutes, that in time would seem

Just long enough to settle hats and say
    I nearly died,
A dozen marriages got under way.
They watched the landscape, sitting side by side
– An Odeon went past, a cooling tower,
And someone running up to bowl – and none
Thought of the others they would never meet
Or how their lives would all contain this hour.
I thought of London spread out in the sun,
Its postal districts packed like squares of wheat:

There we were aimed. And as we raced across
    Bright knots of rail
Past standing Pullmans, walls of blackened moss
Came close, and it was nearly done, this frail
Travelling coincidence; and what it held
Stood ready to be loosed with all the power
That being changed can give. We slowed again,
And as the tightened brakes took hold, there swelled
A sense of falling, like an arrow-shower
Sent out of sight, somewhere becoming rain.

The Slow Train

Millers Dale for Tideswell
Kirby Muxloe
Mow Cop and Scholar Green

No more will I go to Blandford Forum and Mortiehow,
On the slow train from Midsummer Norton and Mumby Row,
No churns, no porter,
No cat on a seat,
At Chorlton-cum-Hardy and Chester-le-Street
We won't be meeting again on the slow train.

I'll travel no more from Littleton Badsey to Openshaw,
At Long Stanton I'll stand well clear of the doors no more,
No whitewashed pebbles,
No up and no down,
From Thornby Four Crosses to Dunstable Town,
I won't be going again on the slow train.

On the main line and the goods siding,
The grass grows high,
At Dog Dyke, Tumby Woodside, and Troublehouse Halt.
The sleepers sleep at Audlem and Ambergate,
No passenger waits on Chittening platform of Cheslyn Hay,
No-one departs, no-one arrives,
From Selby to Goole,
From St. Erth to St. Ives,
They all passed out of our lives,

On the slow train,
On the slow train.
Cockermouth for Buttermere
On the slow train.
Armly Moor Arram
Pye Hill and Somercotes
On the slow train.
Windmill End . . .

The Very Slow Train,

on the downhill stretch,
moves with the speed with which I grew
and with which I will, in my old age, shrink back
towards the warm and waiting ground –
myself a piston on its single push and pull,
among the billions more,
who grind this almost round world round.
And on the flat we slow to an adhered stamp's progress
across its envelope, or so it seems.
Whole yawning generations
come and go between two sleepers here.
And gazing out the window,
I watch a snail dart and flit beside the track.
The snail, which, before we reach our destination,
will have evolved, its descendants inhabiting shells
with living rooms papered in flock.
They'll rest their single feet on poufs.
They'll watch our train pull in
through windows mucus thin.
They'll see ourselves emerge as orbs of shining mind.
Please God, wait for me.

ALAN BROWNJOHN

The Train

The train will come tomorrow year,
The signals clamber into signs,
The gates will open on the track
Where weeds have grown among the lines.

A murmur in the listening air
Besides the heart's emphatic beat
Will rise beyond the junction bridge
Out of the summer's static heat,

And round the distant, anxious bend
Engine and carriages appear.
But on a sultry afternoon
Your waiting hope could turn to fear.

Confronted with achieved desires
You may see nothing more to do
Than shrink from noise and turn away
As every devil thunders through.

WILLIAM WORDSWORTH

On the Projected Kendal and Windermere Railway

Is then no nook of English ground secure
From rash assault? Schemes of retirement sown
In youth, and 'mid the busy world kept pure
As when their earliest flowers of hope were blown,
Must perish; – how can they this blight endure?
And must he too the ruthless change bemoan
Who scorns a false utilitarian lure
'Mid his paternal fields at random thrown?
Baffle the threat, bright Scene, from Orrest-head
Given to the pausing traveller's rapturous glance:
Plead for thy peace, thou beautiful romance
Of nature; and, if human hearts be dead,
Speak, passing winds; ye torrents, with your strong
And constant voice, protest against the wrong.

October 12, 1844.

STATIONS

WALTER DE LA MARE

The Railway Junction

From here through tunnelled gloom the track
Forks into two; and one of these
Wheels onward into darkening hills,
And one toward distant seas.

How still it is; the signal light
At set of sun shines palely green;
A thrush sings; other sound there's none,
Nor traveller to be seen –

Where late there was a throng. And now,
In peace awhile, I sit alone;
Though soon, at the appointed hour,
I shall myself be gone.

But not their way: the bow-legged groom,
The parson in black, the widow and son,
The sailor with his cage, the gaunt
Gamekeeper with his gun,

That fair one, too, discreetly veiled –
All, who so mutely came, and went,
Will reach those far nocturnal hills,
Or shores, ere night is spent.

I nothing know why thus we met –
Their thoughts, their longings, hopes, their fate:

And what shall I remember, except –
The evening growing late –

That here through tunnelled gloom the track
Forks into two; of these
One into darkening hills leads on,
And one toward distant seas?

SIMON ARMITAGE

The Metaphor Now Standing at Platform 8

will separate at Birmingham New Street, and passengers
for the South West who sit for safety reasons in the rear carriage
will find themselves at Shit Creek Central without a paddle
or a valid ticket. No end of fancy talking will save them.

Parents and their children are today invited
to the engine of the metaphor, and may touch the dead man's
handle.
Cow-catchers? Fried bacon on the footplateman's shovel?
People,
please, this is 1990 not the Wild West.

You kids licking the tips of your pencils, I could talk
of the age of steam, riding the great Similitudes
into the record books. Take heart, a boy
could do worse than be a spotter of metaphors.

Here is the buffet car at the centre
of the metaphor, where hot buttered toast
and alcoholic beverages will certainly be mentioned.
In the next breath, lunch will be served.

This is not the allegorical boat train.
This is not the symbolic seaplane.
Madam, life is not a destination but a journey; sweet
that your friends should want to meet you there, but stupid.

Passengers, as part of our Transports of Delight programme
let me welcome this morning's poets. Beginning at the guard's van
they will troubadour the aisle reciting their short but engaging
pieces.
Sir, I understand you have a reservation?

Feet off the seats, please. Lady, for the last time,
extinguish that cigarillo. This is a metaphor I'm running here
not a jamboree, and as soon as we get that straight
we're rolling. Till then, no one goes nowhere.

W. H. AUDEN

Gare du Midi

A nondescript express in from the South,
Crowds round the ticket barrier, a face
To welcome which the mayor has not contrived
Bugles or braid: something about the mouth
Distracts the stray look with alarm and pity.
Snow is falling. Clutching a little case,
He walks out briskly to infect a city
Whose terrible future may have just arrived.

Adlestrop

Yes. I remember Adlestrop –
The name, because one afternoon
Of heat the express-train drew up there
Unwontedly. It was late June.

The steam hissed. Someone cleared his throat.
No one left and no one came
On the bare platform. What I saw
Was Adlestrop – only the name

And willows, willow-herb, and grass,
And meadowsweet, and haycocks dry,
No whit less still and lonely fair
Than the high cloudlets in the sky.

And for that minute a blackbird sang
Close by, and round him, mistier,
Farther and farther, all the birds
Of Oxfordshire and Gloucestershire.

JOHN BETJEMAN

Pershore Station, *or* A Liverish Journey First Class

The train at Pershore station was waiting that Sunday night
Gas light on the platform, in my carriage electric light,
Gas light on frosty evergreens, electric on Empire wood,
The Victorian world and the present in a moment's neighbourhood.
There was no one about but a conscript who was saying good-bye
    to his love
On the windy weedy platform with the sprinkled stars above
When sudden the waiting stillness shook with the ancient spells
Of an older world than all our worlds in the sound of the
    Pershore bells.
They were ringing them down for Evensong in the lighted
    abbey near,
Sounds which had poured through apple boughs for seven
    centuries here.
With Guilt, Remorse, Eternity the void within me fills
And I thought of her left behind me in the Herefordshire hills.
I remembered her defencelessness as I made my heart a stone
Till she wove her self-protection round and left me on my own.
And plunged in a deep self pity I dreamed of another wife
And lusted for freckled faces and lived a separate life.
One word would have made her love me, one word would have
    made her turn
But the word I never murmured and now I am left to burn.
Evesham, Oxford and London. The carriage is new and smart.
I am cushioned and soft and heated with a deadweight in my heart.

WILFRED OWEN

The Send-off

Down the close darkening lanes they sang their way
To the siding-shed,
And lined the train with faces grimly gay.

Their breasts were stuck all white with wreath and spray
As men's are, dead.

Dull porters watched them, and a casual tramp
Stood staring hard,
Sorry to miss them from the upland camp.

Then, unmoved, signals nodded, and a lamp
Winked to the guard.

So secretly, like wrongs hushed-up, they went.
They were not ours:
We never heard to which front these were sent;

Nor there if they yet mock what women meant
Who gave them flowers.

Shall they return to beating of great bells
In wild train-loads?
A few, a few, too few for drums and yells,

May creep back, silent, to village wells,
Up half-known roads.

FRANCES CORNFORD

Parting in Wartime

How long ago Hector took off his plume,
Not wanting that his little son should cry,
Then kissed his sad Andromache goodbye –
And now we three in Euston waiting-room.

THOM GUNN

Berlin in Ruins

Anhalter Bahnhof

It has an edge, or many edges.
The memory that most recurs is
of bronze Imperial fantasies

squirming with plump hauteur on the one
wall of a brown-brick railway station
soon to be reduced. That great ruin

totters beneath associations.
But you encounter a resistance,
and yourself resist. It is at once

unyielding in texture and fertile.
The mind does not rest without peril
among the tarnished blades of laurel:

it may cut on them, it may fester
– until it throbs with a revived fear
of the dark hysteric conqueror

returning from France in triumph as
the hectic that overtakes process,
beneath a silk tent of swastikas.

And fever may descend on the brow
like the high circlet, in whose shadow
the mind awakes, bathed in poison now;

or, harder and sharper than bronze, still
supporting the insupportable,
it may survive its own stiff laurel.

PATRICK MCGUINNESS

Correspondances

The half-hour standstill between Poix-Saint-Hubert
and somewhere else whose name you've never caught
despite forty years of passing it and a little less
of thinking yourself attentive to all that passes you
is time in bas-relief, emphatic in its hollowness:
a rising tide of empty minutes draining
all the station clocks from here to Arlon,

their blank faces hung like moons above the platforms
where sheets of tabulated time contrive to be at once
exact (the 11.27 to Namur)
and untrue (it isn't there).
                    Correspondances
is what they call connecting trains, even when

they don't connect. Even when they don't exist.
But as in Baudelaire's poem, the page
is where they couple, that hub of all encounters,
the clearing in the forest of iron and steam.

Pointed Boots

At three in the morning,
A quietness descends on central railway stations.

A mail van, or an ambulance, may be there;
A man in pointed boots, a Miss Carew.

Quietness keeps them apart,
The quietness that descends on central railway stations.

It is not meant for me.
It is not meant for you.

JOHN MONTAGUE

All Legendary Obstacles

All legendary obstacles lay between
Us, the long imaginary plain,
The monstrous ruck of mountains
And, swinging across the night,
Flooding the Sacramento, San Joaquin,
The hissing drift of winter rain.

All day I waited, shifting
Nervously from station to bar
As I saw another train sail
By, the San Francisco Chief or
Golden Gate, water dripping
From great flanged wheels.

At midnight you came, pale
Above the negro porter's lamp.
I was too blind with rain
And doubt to speak, but
Reached from the platform
Until our chilled hands met.

You had been travelling for days
With an old lady, who marked
A neat circle on the glass
With her glove, to watch us
Move into the wet darkness
Kissing, still unable to speak.

A Station

after Jenő Dsida

An official announcement crackling like deep-fried fat
that our branch-line train would be three hours delayed.
A garbled explanation, some reference to points failure.

And so this Thursday night, I stamp feet on the platform's pier,
venturing to the edge of choppy dark, like a man walking a plank.
Back in the yellow, dank, retch-smelling station building,

I read maps cracked on walls, see pierced hearts squeezed
in felt-tip between names; a revving engine raises,
dashes hopes, abandoning me to loneliness again, a pattern

repeating like the taste of supper in my mouth, thoughts
of betrayal in my mind. The blood is faltering in my veins.
A pale man, slumped near the blinded ticket kiosk, eyes

the clock; a young woman, tightening her veil of silence,
looks aside – it would be good to hear companionable sounds.
No chance. I listen as my inner demons prophecy what cruxes

lie in wait. Telegraph scaffolds line embankments.
Peter could snooze until cock-crow. James drools into
the neat pillow he has made of his scarf. John,

sleeping rough on concrete, keeps watch on his bad dreams.
Restless, I resume my platform vigil, fear streaming down
my forehead in the signal light's unyielding red.

Then, like switching tracks, I start to pray that my train
might never arrive, that my journey be indefinitely delayed,
my forward connections missed, that my cup might pass from me.

LOUIS SIMPSON

The Unwritten Poem

You will never write the poem about Italy.
What Socrates said about love
is true of poetry – where is it?
Not in beautiful faces and distant scenery
but the one who writes and loves.

In your life here, on this street
where the houses from the outside
are all alike, and so are the people.
Inside, the furniture is dreadful –
flock on the walls, and huge color television.

To love and write unrequited
is the poet's fate. Here you'll need
all your ardor and ingenuity.
This is the front and these are the heroes –
a life beginning with 'Hi!' and ending with 'So long!'

You must rise to the sound of the alarm
and march to catch the 6.20 –
watch as they ascend the station platform
and, grasping briefcases, pass beyond your gaze
and hurl themselves into the flames.

Father in the Railway Buffet

What are you doing here, ghost, among these urns,
These film-wrapped sandwiches and help-yourself biscuits,
Upright and grand, with your stick, hat and gloves,
Your breath of eau-de-cologne?

What have you to say to these head-scarfed tea-ladies,
For whom your expensive vowels are exotic as Japan?
Stay, ghost, in your proper haunts, the clubland smokerooms,
Where you know the waiters by name.

You have no place among these damp and nameless.
Why do you walk here? *I came to say goodbye.*
You were ashamed of me for being different.
It didn't matter.

You who never even learned to queue?

IAN HAMILTON

Pretending Not to Sleep

The waiting rooms are full of 'characters'
Pretending not to sleep.
Your eyes are open
But you're far away
At home, *am Rhein*, with mother and the cats.
Your hair grazes my wrist.
My cold hand surprises you.

The porters yawn against the slot-machines
And watch contentedly; they know I've lost.
The last train
Is simmering outside, and overhead
Steam flowers in the station rafters.
Soft flecks of soot begin to settle
On your suddenly outstretched palms.
Your mouth is dry, excited, going home:

The velvet curtains,
Father dead, the road up to the village,
Your hands tightening in the thick fur
Of your mother's Persian, your dreams
Moving through Belgium now, full of your trip.

TONY HARRISON

Changing at York

A directory that runs from B to V,
the Yellow Pages' entries for HOTELS
and TAXIS torn out, the smell of dossers' pee,
saliva in the mouthpiece, whisky smells –
I remember, now I have to phone,
squashing a *Daily Mail* half full of chips,
to tell the son I left at home alone
my train's delayed, and get cut off by the pips,
how, phoning his mother, late, a little pissed,
changing at York; from some place where I'd read,
I used 2p to lie about the train I'd missed
and ten more to talk my way to some girl's bed
and, in this same kiosk with the stale, sour breath
of queuing callers, drunk, cajoling, lying,
consoling his grampa for his granny's death,
how I heard him, for the first time ever, crying.

MICHAEL HOFMANN

Nighthawks

for James Lasdun

Time isn't money, at our age, it's water.
You couldn't say we cupped our hands very tightly . . .
We missed the second-last train, and find ourselves
at the station with half an hour to kill.

The derelicts queue twice round the tearoom.
Outside, the controlled prostitutes move smoothly
through the shoals of men laughing off their fear.
The street-lamps are a dull coral, snakes' heads.

Earlier, I watched a couple over your shoulder.
She was thin, bone-chested, dressed in black lace,
her best feature vines of hair. Blatant, ravenous,
post-coital, they greased their fingers as they ate.

I met a dim acquaintance, a man with the manner
of a laughing-gas victim, rich, frightened and jovial.
Why doesn't everyone wear pink, he squeaked.
Only a couple of blocks are safe in his world.

Now we've arrived at this hamburger heaven,
a bright hole walled with mirrors where our faces show
pale and evacuated in the neon. We spoon our sundaes
from a metal dish. The chopped nuts are poison.

We've been six straight hours together, my friend,
sitting in a shroud of earnestness and misgiving.
Swarthy, big-lipped, suffering, tubercular,
your hollow darkness survives even in this place . . .

The branch-line is under the axe, but it still runs,
rattling and screeching, between the hospital
lit like a toy, and the castellated factory –
a *folie de grandeur* of late capitalism.

The marshalling yard

In the goods yard the tracks are unmarked.
Snow lies, the sky is full of it.
Its hush swells in the dark.

Grasped by black ice on black
a massive noise of breathing
fills the tracks;

cold women, ready for departure
smooth their worn skirts
and ice steals through their hands like children
from whose touch they have already been parted.

Now like a summer
the train comes
beating the platform
with its blue wings.

The women stir. They sigh.
Feet slide
warm on a wooden stairway
then a voice calls and
milk drenched with aniseed
drawls on the walk to school.

At last they leave.
Their breathless neighbours
steal from the woods, the barns,
and tender straw
sticks to their palms.

Friday Night in the Royal Station Hotel

Light spreads darkly downwards from the high
Clusters of lights over empty chairs
That face each other, coloured differently.
Through open doors, the dining-room declares
A larger loneliness of knives and glass
And silence laid like carpet. A porter reads
An unsold evening paper. Hours pass,
And all the salesmen have gone back to Leeds,
Leaving full ashtrays in the Conference Room.

In shoeless corridors, the lights burn. How
Isolated, like a fort, it is –
The headed paper, made for writing home
(If home existed) letters of exile: *Now
Night comes on. Waves fold behind villages.*

DANNIE ABSE

Not Adlestrop

Not Adlestrop, no – besides, the name
hardly matters. Nor did I languish in June heat.
Simply, I stood, too early, on the empty platform,
and the wrong train came in slowly, surprised, stopped.
Directly facing me, from a window,
a very, *very* pretty girl leaned out.

      When I, all instinct,
stared at her, she, all instinct, inclined her head away
as if she'd divined the much married life in me,
or as if she might spot, up platform,
some unlikely familiar.

For my part, under the clock, I continued
my scrutiny with unmitigated pleasure.
And she knew it, she certainly knew it, and would not
glance at me in the silence of not Adlestrop.

      Only when the train heaved noisily, only
when it jolted, when it slid away, only *then*,
daring and secure, she smiled back at my smile,
and I, daring and secure, waved back at her waving.
And so it was, all the way down the hurrying platform
as the train gathered atrocious speed
towards Oxfordshire or Gloucestershire.

The Railroad Station

My nonarrival in the city of N.
took place on the dot.

You'd been alerted
in my unmailed letter.

You were able not to be there
at the agreed-upon time.

The train pulled up at Platform 3.
A lot of people got out.

My absence joined the throng
as it made its way toward the exit.

Several women rushed
to take my place
in all that rush.

Somebody ran up to one of them.
I didn't know him,
but she recognized him
immediately.

While they kissed
with not our lips,

a suitcase disappeared,
not mine.

The railroad station in the city of N.
passed its exam
in objective existence
with flying colors.

The whole remained in place.
Particulars scurried
along the designated tracks.

Even a rendezvous
took place as planned.

Beyond the reach
of our presence.

In the paradise lost
of probability.

Somewhere else.
Somewhere else.
How these little words ring.

UNDERGROUND

EZRA POUND

In a Station of the Metro

The apparition of these faces in the crowd;
Petals on a wet, black bough.

MICHAEL DONAGHY

Poem On The Underground

Sirs, as ancient maps imagine monsters
so London's first anatomical charts
displayed the innards of a vast loud animal;
writhing discrete circulatory systems
venous, arterial, lymphatic, rendered
into District, Piccadilly, Bakerloo . . .
But Harry Beck's map was a circuit diagram
of coloured wires soldered at the stations.
It showed us all we needed then to know,
and knew already, that the city's
an angular appliance of intentions, not
the blood and guts of everything that happens.
Commuters found it 'easier to read'.

My new 3D design improves on Beck,
restoring something of the earlier complexity.
See, here I've drawn the ordinary lines
but crossing these, weaving through the tunnels,
coded beyond the visible spectrum, I've graphed
the vector of today's security alert
due to a suspect package at Victoria,
to the person under a train at Mill Hill East,
with all the circumstantial stops between.

So the vomiting temp in the last train out of Brixton
links to the fingerless busker doing card tricks
making himself invisible to a crowded carriage.

The lines along the third dimension indicate
connections through time: here, the King's Cross fire
leads back to wartime bivouacs on station platforms
and further still, to children singing on a sunlit hill.
Admittedly my design is less accessible than Beck's,
being infinite and imperceptible, but I'm confident,
that given time, the public would embrace it.
I strongly urge the panel to consider my proposal.
Respectfully submitted, May 9, 2003.

SEAMUS HEANEY

District and Circle

Tunes from a tin whistle underground
Curled up a corridor I'd be walking down
To where I knew I was always going to find
My watcher on the tiles, cap by his side,
His fingers perked, his two eyes eyeing me
In an unaccusing look I'd not avoid,
Or not just yet, since both were out to see
For ourselves.
                    As the music larked and capered
I'd trigger and untrigger a hot coin
Held at the ready, but now my gaze was lowered
For was our traffic not in recognition?
Accorded passage, I would re-pocket and nod,
And he, still eyeing me, would also nod.

                    ~

Posted, eyes front, along the dreamy ramparts
Of escalators ascending and descending
To a monotonous slight rocking in the works,
We were moved along, upstanding.
Elsewhere, underneath, an engine powered,
Rumbled, quickened, evened, quieted.
The white tiles gleamed. In passages that flowed
With draughts from cooler tunnels, I missed the light
Of all-overing, long since mysterious day,
Parks at lunchtime where the sunners lay

On body-heated mown grass regardless,
A resurrection scene minutes before
The resurrection, habitués
Of their garden of delights, of staggered summer.

~

Another level down, the platform thronged.
I re-entered the safety of numbers,
A crowd half straggle-ravelled and half strung
Like a human chain, the pushy newcomers
Jostling and purling underneath the vault,
On their marks to be first through the doors,
Street-loud, then succumbing to herd-quiet . . .
Had I betrayed or not, myself or him?
Always new to me, always familiar,
This unrepentant, now repentant turn
As I stood waiting, glad of a first tremor,
Then caught up in the now-or-never whelm
Of one and all the full length of the train.

~

Stepping on to it across the gap,
On to the carriage metal, I reached to grab
The stubby black roof-wort and take my stand
From planted ball of heel to heel of hand
As sweet traction and heavy down-slump stayed me.
I was on my way, well girded, yet on edge,
Spot-rooted, buoyed, aloof,
Listening to the dwindling noises off,
My back to the unclosed door, the platform empty;
And wished it could have lasted,

That long between-times pause before the budge
And glaze-over, when any forwardness
Was unwelcome and bodies readjusted,
Blindsided to themselves and other bodies.

So deeper into it, crowd-swept, strap-hanging,
My lofted arm a-swivel like a flail,
My father's glazed face in my own waning
And craning . . .
             Again the growl
Of shutting doors, the jolt and one-off treble
Of iron on iron, then a long centrifugal
Haulage of speed through every dragging socket.

And so by night and day to be transported
Through galleried earth with them, the only relict
Of all that I belonged to, hurtled forward,
Reflecting in a window mirror-backed
By blasted weeping rock-walls.
                     Flicker-lit.

SEAMUS HEANEY

The Underground

There we were in the vaulted tunnel running,
You in your going-away coat speeding ahead
And me, me then like a fleet god gaining
Upon you before you turned to a reed

Or some new white flower japped with crimson
As the coat flapped wild and button after button
Sprang off and fell in a trail
Between the Underground and the Albert Hall.

Honeymooning, mooning around, late for the Proms,
Our echoes die in that corridor and now
I come as Hansel came on the moonlit stones
Retracing the path back, lifting the buttons

To end up in a draughty lamplit station
After the trains have gone, the wet track
Bared and tensed as I am, all attention
For your step following and damned if I look back.

Comrade Bear

Eh saw um sklent
            fae thi side o meh eh
medved at Sviblovo,
                a bear on an escalator, amid
thi coats of airms, the letters
in anodised Church Slavonic aluminium.

Thi bear descendin thru thi platform
gangin doon wi nae murmel o sang
tae thi hinny belly core
                cucurbit o sweet lava
wi thi glow pollen globes tae licht his wey
tae whaur thi blin bees
                glammach an stir,
lady Cossack insecks wi thir spears
turning thi deid
           owre and owre
                i thi glaizie glaur.

Eh saw thi bear descend tae glowr
at pharaohs and tsars
preservit in glycerine and tar
Triassic in aspic
            Jurassic in amber
borassic i thi braziers and mire.

medved (медведь) – a bear.
sklent, sideways; *murmel*, murmur; *hinny*, honey; *glammach*, snap
at; *glaizie*, glittering, sleek; *glaur*, sticky mud; *borassic*, penniless.

EDWIN MORGAN

The Piranhas

from The Glasgow Subway Poems

Did anyone tell you
that in each subway train
there is one special seat
with a small hole in it
and underneath the seat
is a tank of piranha-fish
which have not been fed
for quite some time.
The fish become agitated
by the shoogling of the train
and jump up through the seat.
The resulting skeletons
of unlucky passengers
turn an honest penny
for the transport executive,
hanging far and wide
in medical schools.

MATTHEW SWEENEY

Tube Ride to Martha's

Before the sirens started, he was late –
late for a dinner at his woman's,
but he'd managed to find a good Rioja
and an excellent excuse: his cat
had burned her tail in the toaster
(this was true) and he'd brought her
to the vet and back in a cab.
He thought about a third cab to Martha's
but funds were low, and the tube ride
was four stops, a half hour with the walks.
He had a thriller in his carrier-bag,
a Ross McDonald, long out of print,
which he opened on the escalator, wanting
it finished tonight. When the smoke came
he hardly noticed, till the black guard
tried to hustle everyone upstairs,
and trains rushed by, without stopping,
and people pushed and screamed.
As the smoke got thicker and blacker
with flames growing fast, he realised
it was over, almost before it had begun.

CHARLES REZNIKOFF

from Jerusalem the Golden

15

In the street I have just left
the small leaves of the trees along the gutter
were steadfast
in the blue heavens.
Now the subway
express
picks up speed
and a wind
blows through the car,
blows dust
on the passengers,
and along the floor
bits of paper –
wrappers of candy,
of gum, tinfoil,
pieces of newspaper. . .

16

Going to work in the subway
this bright May morning
you have put on red slippers;
do they dance behind the counters
in the store, or about the machines
in the shop where you work?

17

Rails in the subway,
what did you know of happiness,
when you were ore in the earth;
now the electric lights shine upon you.

18

Walk about the subway station
in a grove of steel pillars;
how their knobs, the rivet-heads –
unlike those of oaks –
are regularly placed;
how barren the ground is
except here and there on the platform
a flat black fungus
that was chewing-gum.

19   *For an Inscription over the Entrance to
a Subway Station*

This is the gift of Hephaestus, the artificer,
the god men say is lame.

20

In steel clouds
to the sound of thunder
like the ancient gods:
our sky, cement;
the earth, cement;
our trees, steel;
instead of sunshine,

[86]

a light that has no twilight,
neither morning nor evening,
only noon.

Coming up the subway stairs, I thought the moon
only another street-light –
a little crooked.

TRAVELLERS

Love in Vain Blues

And I followed her to the station with a suitcase in my hand.
And I followed her to the station with a suitcase in my hand.
Well, it's hard to tell, it's hard to tell when all your love's in vain.
All my love's in vain.

When the train rolled up to the station I looked her in the eye,
When the train rolled up to the station and I looked her in the eye,
Well, I was lonesome, I felt so lonesome and I could not help but cry.
All my love's in vain.

When the train, it left the station with two lights on behind,
When the train, it left the station with two lights on behind,
Well, the blue light was my blues and the red light was my mind.
All my love's in vain. Ooh, hoo, hoo, Willie Mae.

Oh, hey, hoo, Willie Mae.
Ooh hoo, hoo, wee, oh woe, all my love's in vain.

WENDY COPE

from Strugnell's Sonnets

*At the moment, if you're seen reading poetry
in a train, the carriage empties instantly.*
ANDREW MOTION in a *Guardian* interview

Indeed 'tis true. I travel here and there
On British Rail a lot. I've often said
That if you haven't got the first-class fare
You really need a book of verse instead.
Then, should you find that all the seats are taken,
Brandish your Edward Thomas, Yeats or Pound.
Your fellow-passengers, severely shaken,
Will almost all be loath to stick around.
Recent research in railway sociology
Shows it's best to read the stuff aloud:
A few choice bits from Motion's new anthology
And you'll be lonelier than any cloud.
This stratagem's a godsend to recluses
And demonstrates that poetry has its uses.

Day Return

Your work up north takes longer than you think.
You have to have a drink with a man
who doesn't have a home to go to
and lets his hand fall heavily on your own
in explanation. The train he finds for you
is a mockery of a train
and keeps slipping backwards into wartime obscurity –
blackouts and unexplained halts.

Is it really the same day
you arrived in that northern city in a clean shirt
and walked through sunfilled streets
with half an hour to kill?
You sit in your corner seat
holding your ticket in your hand.
Someone asks if there is a buffet car on the train
and is told he must be joking.

On The Amtrak From Boston To New York City

The white woman across the aisle from me says, 'Look,
look at all the history, that house
on the hill there is over two hundred years old,'
as she points out the window past me

into what she has been taught. I have learned
little more about American history during my few days
back East than what I expected and far less
of what we should all know of the tribal stories

whose architecture is 15,000 years older
than the corners of the house that sits
museumed on the hill. 'Walden Pond,'
the woman on the train asks, 'Did you see Walden Pond?'

and I don't have a cruel enough heart to break
her own by telling her there are five Walden Ponds
on my little reservation out West
and at least a hundred more surrounding Spokane,

the city I pretend to call my home. 'Listen,'
I could have told her. 'I don't give a shit
about Walden. I know the Indians were living stories
around that pond before Walden's grandparents were born

and before his grandparents' grandparents were born.
I'm tired of hearing about Don-fucking-Henley saving it, too,

because that's redundant. If Don Henley's brothers and sisters
and mothers and fathers hadn't come here in the first place

then nothing would need to be saved.'
But I didn't say a word to the woman about Walden
Pond because she smiled so much and seemed delighted
that I thought to bring her an orange juice

back from the food car. I respect elders
of every color. All I really did was eat
my tasteless sandwich, drink my Diet Pepsi
and nod my head whenever the woman pointed out

another little piece of her country's history
while I, as all Indians have done
since this war began, made plans
for what I would do and say the next time

somebody from the enemy thought I was one of their own.

JOHN ASHBERY

Melodic Trains

A little girl with scarlet enameled fingernails
Asks me what time it is – evidently that's a toy wristwatch
She's wearing, for fun. And it is fun to wear other
Odd things, like this briar pipe and tweed coat

Like date-colored sierras with the lines of seams
Sketched in and plunging now and then into unfathomable
Valleys that can't be deduced by the shape of the person
Sitting inside it – me, and just as our way is flat across
Dales and gulches, as though our train were a pencil

Guided by a ruler held against a photomural of the Alps
We both come to see distance as something unofficial
And impersonal yet not without its curious justification
Like the time of a stopped watch – right twice a day.

Only the wait in stations is vague and
Dimensionless, like oneself. How do they decide how much
Time to spend in each? One begins to suspect there's no
Rule or that it's applied haphazardly.

Sadness of the faces of children on the platform,
Concern of the grownups for connections, for the chances
Of getting a taxi, since these have no timetable.
You get one if you can find one though in principle

[96]

You can always find one, but the segment of chance
In the circle of certainty is what gives these leaning
Tower of Pisa figures their aspect of dogged
Impatience, banking forward into the wind.

In short any stop before the final one creates
Clouds of anxiety, of sad, regretful impatience
With ourselves, our lives, the way we have been dealing
With other people up until now. Why couldn't
We have been more considerate? These figures leaving

The platform or waiting to board the train are my brothers
In a way that really wants to tell me why there is so little
Panic and disorder in the world, and so much unhappiness.
If I were to get down now to stretch, take a few steps

In the wearying and world-weary clouds of steam like great
White apples, might I just through proximity and aping
Of postures and attitudes communicate this concern of mine
To them? That their jagged attitudes correspond to mine,

That their beefing strikes answering silver bells within
My own chest, and that I know, as they do, how the last
Stop is the most anxious one of all, though it means
Getting home at last, to the pleasures and dissatisfactions of home?

It's as though a visible chorus called up the different
Stages of the journey, singing about them and being them:
Not the people in the station, not the child opposite me
With currant fingernails, but the windows, seen through,

Reflecting imperfectly, ruthlessly splitting open the bluish
Vague landscape like a zipper. Each voice has its own
Descending scale to put one in one's place at every stage;
One need never not know where one is

Unless one give up listening, sleeping, approaching a small
Western town that is nothing but a windmill. Then
The great fury of the end can drop as the solo
Voices tell about it, wreathing it somehow with an aura

Of good fortune and colossal welcomes from the mayor and
Citizens' committees tossing their hats into the air.
To hear them singing you'd think it had already happened
And we had focused back on the furniture of the air.

Thoughts in a Train

No doubt she is somebody's mistress,
  With that Greta Garbo hair,
As she sits, mascara-lidded,
  In the corner seat over there.

But why, if she's somebody's mistress,
  Is she travelling up in a Third?
Her luggage is leather, not plastic,
  Her jewelry rich and absurd.

'Oh I am nobody's mistress:
  The jewels I wear, you see,
Were, like this leather luggage,
  A present from Mummy to me.

'If you want to get on with the Government,
  You've got to be like it, I've heard;
So I've booked my suite in the Ritz Hotel
  and I'm travelling up in a Third.'

JOHN FULLER

In a Railway Compartment

Oxford to London, 1884:
Against the crimson arm-rest leaned a girl
Often, holding a muff, twisting a curl,
Drumming her heels in boredom on the floor
Until a white-haired gentleman who saw
She hated travelling produced a case
Of puzzles: 'Seven Germans run a race . . .
Unwind this maze, escape the lion's paw . . .
The princess must be lowered by her hair . . .'
The train entered a tunnel, shrieking, all
The lights went out and when he took her hand
She was the princess in the tower and
A lion faced her on the moonlit wall
Who roared and reached and caught and held her there.

ELMA MITCHELL

The Passenger Opposite

British Rail

Everything falls asleep with sleep
— The wariness, the will —
It's hard to loathe a sleeping face
Lapsed back into a state of grace,
    Naked, relaxed and still.

Even the hair is childish now,
    Rumpled and damp and young,
The teeth unclenched, the hands let loose,
Both smile and frown gone out of use,
    No message from the tongue.

The mouth has slackened, and the chin
    Given up its thrust and drive,
The eyes have left their sentry box,
The ears have closed their subtle locks.
    Content to be alive

Just breathing; and the eyelashes
    Are delicate, and long,
They stoop, and soothe the fretted cheek
Which knows no words nor need to speak,
    No scope for going wrong.

This is the sleep of train, and plane,
　Of hammock, bunk and pram,
Deck-chair and hospital and cot,
Of slaked desire, of world-forgot,
　Of I-Am-That-I-Am.

And if the shoulder's tapped, or shouts
　Disturb the rhythmic bliss,
Will the face resurrect its fears,
Its irritations and its years
　Or smile, and shape a kiss?

Here is my stop. I must get out
　And cannot answer this.

DOUGLAS DUNN

Renfrewshire Traveller

Home rain, an aerial night-Clyde,
Spray of recollection
And my only appropriate welcome.

Have I come back?
It was dark
Through Kilmarnock,

Johnny Walker blinked
Imperfectly; history
Is whisky, *lacrimae rerum.*

Have I come back?
I am Scots, a tartan tin box
Of shortbread in a delicatessen of cheddars

And southern specialties.
I am full of poison.
Each crumb of me is a death,

Someone you never see again
After funerals in the rain.
Men who return wearing black ties,

Men who return having looked for work –
Hear them, their Glasgow accents
In the night of high-rise

Skyward tenements, railway platforms,
The accents of rain and arguments.
What have I come to?

Not this. Not this
Slow afright over rails,
This ache in a buffet of empty beer-cans.

This wiping of windows to see a city
Rise from its brilliant lack,
Its fixtures in transparent butter.

Not this visitor
To a place of relatives,
A place of names.

PAUL DURCAN

Tullynoe: Tête-à-Tête in the Parish Priest's Parlour

'Ah, he was a grand man.'
'He was: he fell out of the train going to Sligo.'
'He did: he thought he was going to the lavatory.'
'He did: in fact he stepped out the rear door of the train.'
'He did: God, he must have got an awful fright.'
'He did: he saw that it wasn't the lavatory at all.'
'He did: he saw that it was the railway tracks going away
    from him.'
'He did: I wonder if . . . but he was a grand man.'
'He was: he had the most expensive Toyota you can buy.'
'He had: well, it was only beautiful.'
'It was: he used to have an Audi.'
'He had: as a matter of fact he used to have two Audis.'
'He had: and then he had an Avenger.'
'He had: and then he had a Volvo.'
'He had: in the beginning he had a lot of Volkses.'
'He had: he was a great man for the Volkses.'
'He was: did he once have an Escort?'
'He had not: he had a son a doctor.'
'He had: and he had a Morris Minor too.'
'He had: he had a sister a hairdresser in Kilmallock.'
'He had: he had another sister a hairdresser in Ballybunion.'
'He had: he was put in a coffin which was put in his father's cart.'
'He was: his lady wife sat on top of the coffin driving the donkey.'

'She did: Ah, but he was a grand man.'
'He was: he was a grand man . . .'
'Good night, Father.'
'Good night, Mary.'

Corner Seat

Suspended in a moving night
The face in the reflected train
Looks at first sight as self-assured
As your own face – But look again:

Windows between you and the world
Keep out the cold, keep out the fright;
Then why does your reflection seem
So lonely in the moving night?

DAN PAGIS

Written in Pencil in the Sealed Freight Car

Here, in this carload, I, Eve, with my
son Abel. If you see my older boy,
Cain, the son of Adam, tell him that I

LES MURRAY

Troop Train Returning

Beyond the Divide
the days become immense,
beyond our war
in the level lands of wheat,
the things that we defended are still here,
the willow-trees pruned neatly cattle-high,
the summer roads where far-back bullock drays
foundered in earth and mouldered into yarns.
From a ringbarked tree, as we go cheering by
a tower and a whirlwind of white birds,
as we speed by
with a whistle for the plains.

On kitbags in the aisle, old terrors doze,
clumsy as rifles in a peacetime train.
Stopped at a siding
under miles of sun,
I watch a friend I mightn't see again
shyly shake hands, becoming a civilian,
and an old Ford truck
receding to the sky.

I walk about. The silo, tall as Time,
casts on bright straws its coldly southward shade.

All things are spaced out here
each in its value.

The pepper-trees beside the crossroads pub
are dim with peace,
pumpkins are stones
in fields so loosely green.

In a little while, I'll be afraid to look
out for my house and the people that I love,
they have been buried in the moon so long.

Beyond all wars
in the noonday lands of wheat,
the whistle summons shouters from the bar,
refills the train with jokes and window noise.
This perfect plain
casts out the things we've done
as we jostle here, relaxed as farmers, smoking,
held at this siding
till the red clicks green.

On the Train Between Wellington and Shrewsbury

The process starts –
on the rails pigs' blood,
lambs' blood in the trees

With a red tail
through the slab-white sky
the blood bird flies

This man beside me
is offering friendly
sandwiches of speech:
he's slaughtered twenty pigs
this morning –
                              he takes away
the sins of the word

I can smell his jacket,
it's tripe coloured,
old tripe,
drained-out, veteran tripe
that has digested the world

I shut my eyes on
his lullaby of tripe
and the blood goes back to bed

(Someone's got to do it
and I'm grateful
and my neighbour's grateful
and we say so,
but thank God it's only
fourteen minutes to Shrewsbury)

Fourteen minutes to consider
the girl reading Scott Fitzgerald –
she has a red cashmere top
bright as a butcher's window

Shut out the sun and the cameras –
I want to talk to a doctor
about Circe's magic circle –
'you see, it was on the woman herself
the bristles sprang
and the truffle-hunting tongue'

What is it makes my penis
presentable?
hot blood –
enough of it, in the right place

With such red cheeks
my interlocutor from the abbatoirs
must have hypertension

On his knees he has
a lumpish parcel, well-knotted
with white string –
it makes all the difference
when you know it's really fresh

[112]

At one time our species
always had it fresh;
one time there were no cashmere tops
or butcher's shops

It consoles me that poems
bring nothing about,
it hurts me that poems
do so little

I was born after
man invented meat
and a shepherd invented poetry

At a time when there are only
fourteen killing minutes
between Wellington and Shrewsbury.

JEAN SPRACKLAND

The Stopped Train

She stands and knows herself for the first time.
This recognition comes to each of us

sooner or later. When a baby meets a mirror
it enters this same state of rapture.
That's how the train is: stunned
and passionate. She looks, and sees

energy, will, destiny. Sees that she
touches the rails, but is not the rails,
brushes the overhead lines and drinks in power,
is headstrong and pioneering.

Inside, passengers cram the corridors,
sucking ice-cubes, taking turns at the windows.
A woman shouts: Why must you all be so *British*?
The carriage is brash with daylight

like a terrible living-room
filling up with unsaid things:
no one can get a signal here
in this nondescript England of

sly ditches and flat fields, where some
experiment must be taking place and
the only thing moving between the trees is
shadow. This is the Interior,

and if they were to smash the glass with a shoe,
jump down onto the track, set off in a somewhere direction,
they would be struck down
like stranded motorists in Death Valley.

The train has forgotten them.
She is accounting for herself:
steel, glass, plastic, nylon,
an audit of chips and circuits.

She stands and ticks,
letting the heat leak and equalise.

Toilet

I wonder will I speak to the girl
sitting opposite me on this train.
I wonder will my mouth open and say,
'Are you going all the way
to Newcastle?' or 'Can I get you a coffee?'
Or will it simply go 'aaaaah'
as if it had a mind of its own?

Half closing eggshell blue eyes,
she runs her hand through her hair
so that it clings to the carriage cloth,
then slowly frees itself.
She finds a brush and her long fair hair
flies back and forth like an African fly-whisk,
making me feel dizzy.

Suddenly, without warning,
she packs it all away in a rubber band
because I have forgotten to look out
the window for a moment.
A coffee is granted permission
to pass between her lips
and does so eagerly, without fuss.

A tunnel finds us looking out the window
into one another's eyes. She leaves her seat,
but I know that she likes me

because the light saying 'TOILET'
has come on, a sign that she is lifting
her skirt, taking down her pants
and peeing all over my face.

RUTH STONE

from Who is the Widow's Muse?

The widow likes to ride on trains.
Trains are phallic symbols.
The engineer is probably on crack.
His speed outruns the antiquated equipment.
These trains were built for middle-aged engineers.
Once she and her husband
were fooling around on a train.
They were trying to torment
four old men playing cards.
The men's eyes were heavy lidded.
They looked at their hands.
Could the widow's muse be carnal?
Could she have hot pants?

ROBERT CRAWFORD

The Railway Library

Grass is growing through the disused lines
Of *Marmion* and *Martin Rattler*. You could pick up a book
At any station, racing through its chapters
In a slipcase of steam until your destination
Broke off the story. Rochester met Jane Eyre
At Falkirk High; Bram Stoker's action plunged
Through mile-long tunnels; *The Moonstone* gleamed in Paisley.
Women and men bought tickets for good books
That sped home, thundering across the points
Where readers clutched their seats. A suffragette
Sits in her first-class carriage in the cells
Of Monte Cristo; haar and sunlight bleach
High seas off Fife. She vanishes in fog at Leuchars,
Never reads on, still haunted by that picture
Of stone being scraped away and a voice speaking
Through solid wall. Holmes hails a hansom cab
On the poisoner's track in Kelso. Hunched inside
Self-induced personal stereo, sleuthing readers
Read past each other as the four o'clock
Overtakes the mail train, late. Impatient Crewe passengers
For Stevenson are out of luck – his adventures
All borrowed by shy children travelling north
Kidnapped by *Treasure Island.* Books circulate
From Kyle to Wigton; returns, reissued through
First, second, third, get beerstained, reek of cigars.
Some essays outlast viaducts. Folk come

Borrowing words, remembering, misremembering.
After the stock is scrapped, lines uneconomic,
Narratives run unhindered, mothers and daughters
Climb on board, or jump from the moving text
With hankies at their wrists and *Quo Vadis?*

IAN DUHIG

Jericho Shandy

The surrealist machine is more often than
not a nonfunctional machine
SARA DANIUS, *The Senses of Modernism*

Returning from the anniversary
event for Sterne at Bradford Library,
a theft of signal wire maroons his train
beside the Kirkstall Abbey points for Leeds,
a name which sounds a pun, but not to him.
He's feeling hemmed-in by the open space,
a paradoxophobia mixed with . . .
he wonders what word would mean 'fear of nature' –
gaiaphobia? or start with 'pan-',
as in panic, as in panic attack?
He notes Cornell alarm chains under glass,
a hammer under glass for breaking glass.
This Bradford route's a sideline to a sideline,
sidelined now, reflecting on itself,
he thinks, a black-silk-hatted parody,
a *Soft Cell* synth man who only plays
recessionals on his harmonium
as doors close on the coffin and the flames.
He checks the carriage doors. They're locked, of course.
He notes the engine idles in iambics,
growing more insistent all the time.
Distraction from distraction's what he needs;
he thinks of Henry 'Box' Brown, escaped slave,

who recreated on this line his flight
to Northern freedom from Virginia,
and then of Earnshaw, the unescaped artist,
boxmaker, anarchist, who rode here
on his famed Surrealist Expeditions,
now travelling just as fast, although he's dead,
as this steel coffin with an Abbey view.
There's no-one's in his carriage. Or the next,
bar one slumped goth, a daywalker in shades.
He sees the guard is smoking down the track.
Reminded of that traveller's tale from Twain
with mummies fuelling Egyptian trains,
he opens all the carriage windows wide
then gets a head of steam up for himself.
The flesh is grass that fuels his Proto Pipe,
distraction engine of the connoisseur;
a locomotive run on loco weed,
but pocket-sized, its firebox solid brass
with built-in poker, tar-trap, sliding smoke-cap –
Ceci n'est pas une pipe, but art to him
from stem to Sternesque incurled spinning smoke
that rhymes with wire abandoned by the thieves
to kink and bite its tail and arabesque
like drawings of Trim's gestures with his stick.
He draws until his head begins to spin,
thinks Northern Lights a good name for this grass . . .
When straight, he'd kill time on another line
by taking phone cold callers for a ride;
A timeshare? Great! But let's consider time!
He'd fugue on monastery prayer-routines
and Mumford's view their strictness gave the West
its grounding in machine-age discipline,
or Mrs Shandy winding up her husband;

Marx on clockless works; Toussaint L'Ouverture,
his gold watch stolen, exiled in the Jura,
where, in good time, the local watchmakers
would teach Kropotkin real-life anarchism . . .
None laughed, their English often second-hand,
commission making up their sweatshop pay,
his bourgeois deviationism stale,
reduced as one of Bennett's Talking Heads.
But now he listens with intensity
to sounds a swift makes harvesting the sky,
worms churning willowherb and meadowsweet,
the bull chained by its nose to a cartwheel,
a punky sun turning its wooden dial . . .
A tyre's soft watch drips slowly on a tree;
inside, paranoia's less critical
than *tumultuosissimamente*:
he's sure he's suffering Karmic punishment
for keeping hands from working in real life,
his Chinese watch, where copper scrap winds up,
the Golden Virginia in all those joints . . .
The robot heartbeat of the engine turns
to footsteps at his back, death in high heels,
while Kirkstall Abbey melts to Auden's face:
Stop all the clocks, cut off the telephone,
it says to Alan Bennett, Poetry?
But that's found far from outskirts such as these!
Remembering that Bennett lived near Troy,
by Horsforth Station, he thinks of Irwin,
Hector's foe, who lives there in the screenplay
though *Somewhere on the outskirts* on the stage;
then Bennett quoting Eliot on walls;
the History Boys against the National wall
on the book cover Darren Wall designed . . .

Convinced he's trapped now for eternity,
he thinks this page's walls are closing in,
then closes his own eyes to find himself
in his personal page 73:
he dreams evolved new fish will one day find
his cage of bones in the train's rusted cage
with Northern Lights' seeds growing through his ribs
a post-historic forest coast to coast,
his Proto Pipe all protozoic slime . . .
He shudders, then forgets why, at what.
He wonders if the goth brought chocolate.

THOMAS MCCARTHY

The Emigration Trains

A pound-note was the best kind of passport
In those days, so I held my pound tightly
After my mother turned away. Idlers
Waved farewell from Ferrybank corners.
There was nothing heroic about my
Going, nothing like a political destiny –
I'd just wasted a summer standing round
Until a job came up on the Underground.

I felt like a vagrant, destitute, until
At Waterford Station I realized
My good luck: I owned a suitcase of card
While others carried mere bundles of cloth.
At Kilkenny every carriage was filled
To the door. One mother's last grip held fast
Despite the moving train, the rising glass.
For some it was the last touch of a child.

There was nothing pathetic about this;
Even the suffering Jews had kept a brave face.
We had our own State; a place to leave from –
Now the emigrant ship was like a big town:
That night it was Clonmel or Cappoquin,
With bars open, arguments outdoors
And politics racing through bleak corridors.

We were heading for England and the world
At war. Neutrality we couldn't afford.
I thought I would spend two years away
But in the end the two became twenty.
Within hours we'd reach the junction at Crewe
And sample powdered eggs from the menu,
As well as doodlebugs falling nearby;
All that fatal traffic of an alien sky.

I was so raw and Irish at the time
They said that shamrocks grew out of my ears.
I wasn't alone with my homesick mind:
When we sailed into Holyhead our tears
Made a pathetic sea. One labourer's voice
Rose out of the ship, like a skylark's,
Singing *Kevin Barry, Kevin Barry*.
His song became our night-cry at the dock.

Couchette

With my wife, son, daughter in layers up the walls
This room on wheels has become the family vault.
They have fallen asleep, dreams stopping and starting
As my long coffin wobbles on the top couchette.
Shunted down a siding, we shall wait for centuries
Before hurtling to places we have never seen.
No more than a blink of light, a tinkle of bangles,
The old woman who joins us at Turin will leave
Crusts and a plastic bottle of mineral water.
Soon her space will be taken by a younger lady
We met four thousand years ago in Fiesole,
Her face still to be uncovered, and at her feet
A pet cat who has also been wrapped in bandages.

NORMAN MACCAIG

Sleeping compartment

I don't like this, being carried sideways
through the night. I feel wrong and helpless – like
a timber broadside in a fast stream.

Such a way of moving may suit
that odd snake the sidewinder
in Arizona: but not me in Perthshire.

I feel at rightangles to everything,
a crossgrain in existence. – It scrapes
the top of my head and my footsoles.

To forget outside is no help either –
then I become a blockage
in the long gut of the train.

I try to think I'm an Alice in Wonderland
mountaineer bivouacked
on a ledge five feet high.

It's no good. I go sidelong.
I rock sideways . . . I draw in my feet
to let Aviemore pass.

LOUISE GLÜCK

The Chicago Train

Across from me the whole ride
Hardly stirred: just Mister with his barren
Skull across the arm-rest while the kid
Got his head between his mama's legs and slept. The poison
That replaces air took over.
And they sat – as though paralysis preceding death
Had nailed them there. The track bent south.
I saw her pulsing crotch . . . the lice rooted in that baby's hair.

Figure of Eight

In the top and front of a bus, eager to meet his fate,
He pressed with foot and mind to gather speed,
Then, when the lights were changing, jumped and hurried,
Though dead on time, to the meeting place agreed,
But there was no one there. He chose to wait.
No one came. He need not perhaps have worried.

Whereas today in the rear and gloom of a train,
Loath, loath to meet his fate, he cowers and prays
For some last-minute hitch, some unheard-of abdication,
But, winding up the black thread of his days,
The wheels roll on and make it all too plain
Who will be there to meet him at the station.

Yes

I'm drinking in the 7-Up bottle-green eyes of the barmaid
On the Enterprise express – bottles and glasses clinking
  each other –
When the train slows with a noise like Schweppes and halts just
  outside Dundalk.
Not that unwontedly, since we're no strangers to the border bomb.
As the Belfast accent of the tannoy tells us what is happening

I'm about to quote from Bashō's *The Narrow Road to the Deep
  North* –
Blossoming mushroom: from some unknown tree a leaf has stuck to it –
When it goes off and we're thrown out of kilter. My mouth is full
Of broken glass and quinine as everything reverses South.

GRETE TARTLER

Orient Express

Nearly asleep, I'm reading the Desert Fathers.
There are towns, turquoise plains;
at stations I hear announcements in unknown languages.
A man in my compartment was in the war;
he used to play the trumpet.
The woman next to me is crocheting (knots
between good and bad, between truth and falsehood).
It's as if I'm conducting the rhythmic pulse of the train,
the chorus of those who are staying awake
for fear of the dawn.
Once, on holiday in the mountains,
I heard this train go by,
the one I'm on today;
someone told a story about the snake that sucked from a cow:
the men found it asleep among the rocks
and struck it with an axe;
milk flowed from it as if from a cask.
Now over the hills, over the acid waters,
over the Greenpeace ships, over the explosions,
the small publicity, the smog, the dried-up springs,
milk flows in waves.
I feel it taking the form of hills,
the form of the brain:
dawn flows into it without filling it;
dawn leaves it without emptying it.

translated by Fleur Adcock

The Way My Mother Speaks

I say her phrases to myself
in my head
or under the shallows of my breath,
restful shapes moving.
The day and ever. The day and ever.

The train this slow evening
goes down England
browsing for the right sky,
too blue swapped for a cool grey.
For miles I have been saying
What like is it
the way I say things when I think.
Nothing is silent. Nothing is not silent.
What like is it.

Only tonight
I am happy and sad
like a child
who stood at the end of summer
and dipped a net
in a green, erotic pond. *The day
and ever. The day and ever.*
I am homesick, free, in love
with the way my mother speaks.

NIGHT

The Midnight Special

Well you wake up in the mornin', you hear the work bell ring
And they march you to the table to see the same old thing.
Ain't no food upon the table and no pork up in the pan.
But you better not complain boy, you get in trouble with the man.

Let the Midnight Special shine a light on me,
Let the Midnight Special shine a light on me,
Let the Midnight Special shine a light on me,
Let the Midnight Special shine a everlovin' light on me.

Yonder come miss Rosie, how in the world did you know?
By the way she wears her apron, and the clothes she wore.
Umbrella on her shoulder, piece of paper in her hand;
She come to see the gov'nor, she wants to free her man.

Let the Midnight Special shine a light on me,
Let the Midnight Special shine a light on me,
Let the Midnight Special shine a light on me,
Let the Midnight Special shine a everlovin' light on me.

If you're ever in Houston, well, you better do the right;
You better not gamble there, you better not fight at all
Or the sheriff will grab ya and the boys will bring you down.
The next thing you know, boy, Oh! You're prison bound.

Let the Midnight Special shine a light on me,
Let the Midnight Special shine a light on me,

Let the Midnight Special shine a light on me,
Let the Midnight Special shine a everlovin' light on me.

Let the Midnight Special shine a light on me,
Let the Midnight Special shine a light on me,
Let the Midnight Special shine a light on me,
Let the Midnight Special shine a everlovin' light on me

T. S. ELIOT

Skimbleshanks: the Railway Cat

There's a whisper down the line at 11.39
When the Night Mail's ready to depart,
Saying 'Skimble where is Skimble has he gone to hunt the thimble?
We must find him or the train can't start.'
All the guards and all the porters and the stationmaster's
    daughters
They are searching high and low,
Saying 'Skimble where is Skimble for unless he's very nimble
Then the Night Mail just can't go.'
At 11.42 then the signal's overdue
And the passengers are frantic to a man –
Then Skimble will appear and he'll saunter to the rear:
He's been busy in the luggage van!
    He gives one flash of his glass-green eyes
        And the signal goes 'All Clear !'
    And we're off at last for the northern part
        Of the Northern Hemisphere!

You may say that by and large it is Skimble who's in charge
Of the Sleeping Car Express.
From the driver and the guards to the bagmen playing cards
He will supervise them all, more or less.
Down the corridor he paces and examines all the faces
Of the travellers in the First and in the Third;
He establishes control by a regular patrol
And he'd know at once if anything occurred.

He will watch you without winking and he sees what you are
        thinking
And it's certain that he doesn't approve
Of hilarity and riot, so the folk are very quiet
When Skimble is about and on the move.
    You can play no pranks with Skimbleshanks!
        He's a Cat that cannot be ignored;
        So nothing goes wrong on the Northern Mail
            When Skimbleshanks is aboard.

Oh it's very pleasant when you have found your little den
With your name written up on the door.
And the berth is very neat with a newly folded sheet
And there's not a speck of dust on the floor.
There is every sort of light – you can make it dark or bright;
There's a button that you turn to make a breeze.
There's a funny little basin you're supposed to wash your face in
And a crank to shut the window if you sneeze.
Then the guard looks in politely and will ask you very brightly
'Do you like your morning tea weak or strong?'
But Skimble's just behind him and was ready to remind him.
For Skimble won't let anything go wrong.
    And when you creep into your cosy berth
        And pull up the counterpane,
    You ought to reflect that it's very nice
    To know that you won't be bothered by mice –
    You can leave all that to the Railway Cat,
        The Cat of the Railway Train!

In the watches of the night he is always fresh and bright;
Every now and then he has a cup of tea
With perhaps a drop of Scotch while he's keeping on the watch,
Only stopping here and there to catch a flea.

You were fast asleep at Crewe and so you never knew
That he was walking up and down the station;
You were sleeping all the while he was busy at Carlisle,
Where he greets the stationmaster with elation.
But you saw him at Dumfries, where he summons the police
If there's anything they ought to know about:
When you get to Gallowgate there you do not have to wait –
For Skimbleshanks will help you to get out!
   He gives you a wave of his long brown tail
      Which says: 'I'll see you again!
   You'll meet without fail on the Midnight Mail
      The Cat of the Railway Train.'

W. H. AUDEN

Night Mail

(*Commentary for a G. P. O. Film*)

I

This is the Night Mail crossing the Border,
Bringing the cheque and the postal order,

Letters for the rich, letters for the poor,
The shop at the corner, the girl next door.

Pulling up Beattock, a steady climb:
The gradient's against her, but she's on time.

Past cotton-grass and moorland boulder,
Shovelling white steam over her shoulder,

Snorting noisily, she passes
Silent miles of wind-bent grasses.

Birds turn their heads as she approaches,
Stare from bushes at her blank-faced coaches.

Sheep-dogs cannot turn her course;
They slumber on with paws across.

In the farm she passes no one wakes,
But a jug in a bedroom gently shakes.

II

Dawn freshens. Her climb is done.
Down towards Glasgow she descends,
Towards the steam tugs yelping down a glade of cranes,
Towards the fields of apparatus, the furnaces
Set on the dark plain like gigantic chessmen.
All Scotland waits for her:
In dark glens, beside pale-green lochs,
Men long for news.

III

Letters of thanks, letters from banks,
Letters of joy from girl and boy,
Receipted bills and invitations
To inspect new stock or to visit relations,
And applications for situations,
And timid lovers' declarations,
And gossip, gossip from all the nations,
News circumstantial, news financial,
Letters with holiday snaps to enlarge in,
Letters with faces scrawled on the margin,
Letters from uncles, cousins and aunts,
Letters to Scotland from the South of France,
Letters of condolence to Highlands and Lowlands,
Written on paper of every hue,
The pink, the violet, the white and the blue,
The chatty, the catty, the boring, the adoring,
The cold and official and the heart's outpouring,
Clever, stupid, short and long,
The typed and the printed and the spelt all wrong.

IV

Thousands are still asleep,
Dreaming of terrifying monsters
Or a friendly tea beside the band in Cranston's or Crawford's:
Asleep in working Glasgow, asleep in well-set Edinburgh,
Asleep in granite Aberdeen,
They continue their dreams,
But shall wake soon and hope for letters,
And none will hear the postman's knock
Without a quickening of the heart.
For who can bear to feel himself forgotten?

The Missed Train

How I was caught
Hieing home, after days of allure,
And forced to an inn – small, obscure –
    At the junction, gloom-fraught.

How civil my face
To get them to chamber me there –
A roof I had scorned, scarce aware
    That it stood at the place.

And how all the night
I had dreams of the unwitting cause
Of my lodgment. How lonely I was;
    How consoled by her sprite!

Thus onetime to me . . .
Dim wastes of dead years bar away
Then from now. But such happenings to-day
    Fall to lovers, may be!

Years, years as shoaled seas,
Truly, stretch now between! Less and less
Shrink the visions then vast in me. – Yes,
    Then in me: Now in these.

The Tay Bridge Disaster

Beautiful Railway Bridge of the Silv'ry Tay!
Alas! I am very sorry to say
That ninety lives have been taken away
On the last Sabbath day of 1879,
Which will be remember'd for a very long time.

'Twas about seven o'clock at night,
And the wind it blew with all its might,
And the rain came pouring down,
And the dark clouds seem'd to frown,
And the Demon of the air seem'd to say –
'I'll blow down the Bridge of Tay.'

When the train left Edinburgh
The passengers' hearts were light and felt no sorrow,
But Boreas blew a terrific gale,
Which made their hearts for to quail,
And many of the passengers with fear did say –
'I hope God will send us safe across the Bridge of Tay.'

But when the train came near to Wormit Bay,
Boreas he did loud and angry bray,
And shook the central girders of the Bridge of Tay
On the last Sabbath day of 1879,
Which will be remember'd for a very long time.

So the train sped on with all its might,
And Bonnie Dundee soon hove in sight,
And the passengers' hearts felt light,
Thinking they would enjoy themselves on the New Year,
With their friends at home they lov'd most dear,
And wish them all a happy New Year.

So the train mov'd slowly along the Bridge of Tay,
Until it was about midway,
Then the central girders with a crash gave way,
And down went the train and passengers into the Tay!
The Storm Fiend did loudly bray,
Because ninety lives had been taken away,
On the last Sabbath day of 1879,
Which will be remember'd for a very long time.

As soon as the catastrophe came to be known
The alarm from mouth to mouth was blown,
And the cry rang out all o'er the town,
Good Heavens! the Tay Bridge is blown down,
And a passenger train from Edinburgh,
Which fill'd all the people's hearts with sorrow,
And made them for to turn pale,
Because none of the passengers were sav'd to tell the tale
How the disaster happen'd on the last Sabbath day of 1879
Which will be remember'd for a very long time.

It must have been an awful sight,
To witness in the dusky moonlight,
While the Storm Fiend did laugh, and angry did bray,
Along the Railway Bridge of the Silv'ry Tay.
Oh! ill-fated Bridge of the Silv'ry Tay,
I must now conclude my lay

By telling the world fearlessly without the least dismay,
That your central girders would not have given way,
At least many sensible men do say,
Had they been supported on each side with buttresses,
At least many sensible men confesses,
For the stronger we our houses do build,
The less chance we have of being killed.

Travel

The railroad track is miles away,
   And the day is loud with voices speaking,
Yet there isn't a train goes by all day
   But I hear its whistle shrieking.

All night there isn't a train goes by,
   Though the night is still for sleep and dreaming,
But I see its cinders red on the sky,
   And hear its engine steaming.

My heart is warm with the friends I make,
   And better friends I'll not be knowing;
Yet there isn't a train I wouldn't take,
   No matter where it's going.

PAUL MULDOON

The Train

I've been trying, my darling, to explain
to myself how it is that some freight train
loaded with ballast so a track may rest
easier in its bed should be what's roused

us both from ours, tonight as every night,
despite its being miles off and despite
our custom of putting to the very
back of the mind all that's customary

and then, since it takes forever to pass
with its car after car of coal and gas
and salt and wheat and rails and railway ties,

how it seems determined to give the lie
to the notion, my darling,
that we, not it, might be the constant thing.

Mystery Train

Train arrive 16 coaches long
Train arrive 16 coaches long
Well that long black train
Got my baby and gone

Train train rolling round the bend
Train train rolling round the bend
Well it took my baby
Away from me again

Come down to the station
Meet my baby at the gate
Asked the station master
If the train's running late
He said 'If you're a-waiting
on the 444
I hate to tell you son
That train don't stop here anymore'

Train train rolling down down the line
Train train rolling down the line
Well it took my baby
And left poor me behind

Heard that whistle blowing
It was the middle of the night

When I got down to the station
The train was pulling out of sight

Mystery train smoking down the track
Mystery train smoking down the track
Well I don't want no ride
Just bring my baby back

At the Train Museum

Topeka . . . Junction City . . .
Santa Fe. The places
the imagination takes us
are simply these.
All . . . Points . . . East
the conductor calls
in that old plainchant

and a girl with a suitcase
steals down the porch stairs.
Rivers . . . Bridges . . . Cornfields
with stalks as tasseled
as the plaited hair of children
all over Kansas, falling asleep
to the loon-like call

of trains. I board
one more time, sensing
the quicksilver tracks,
how they branch towards a future
where I've long since
been carried, swaying
and only half awake.

Limited

I am riding on a limited express, one of the crack trains of
the nation.
Hurtling across the prairie into blue haze and dark air go
fifteen all-steel coaches holding a thousand people.
(All the coaches shall be scrap and rust and all the men
and women laughing in the diners and sleepers shall
pass to ashes.)
I ask a man in the smoker where he is going and he
answers: 'Omaha.'

DAVE SMITH

Cumberland Station

Gray brick, ash, hand-bent railings, steps so big
it takes hours to mount them, polished oak
pews holding slim hafts of sun, and one
splash of the *Pittsburgh Post-Gazette*. The man
who left Cumberland gone, come back, no job
anywhere. I come here alone, shaken
the way I came years ago to ride down
mountains in Big Daddy's cab. He was
the first set cold in the black meadow.

Six rows of track, photographed, gleam, rippling
like water on walls where famous engineers steam, half
submerged in frothing crowds with something
to celebrate and plenty to eat. One engineer
takes children for a free ride, a frolic
like an earthquake. Ash cakes their hair.
I am one of those who walked uphill
through flowers of soot to zing
scared to death into the world.

Now whole families afoot cruise South Cumberland
for something to do, no jobs, no money for bars,
the old stories cracked like wallets.

This time there's no fun in coming back. The second
death. My roundhouse uncle coughed his youth

into a gutter. His son slid on the ice,
losing his need to drink himself
stupidly dead. In this vaulted hall
I think of all the dirt poured down
from shovels and trains and empty pockets.
I stare into the huge malignant headlamps
circling the gray walls and catch a stuttered
glimpse of faces stunned like deer on a track.

Churning through the inner space of this godforsaken
wayside, I feel the ground try to upchuck and I dig
my fingers in my temples to bury a child
diced on a cowcatcher, a woman smelling
alkaline from washing out the soot.
Where I stood in that hopeless, hateful room
will not leave me. The scarf of smoke I saw
over a man's shoulder runs through me
like the sored Potomac River.

Grandfather, you ask why I don't visit you
now you have escaped the ticket-seller's cage
to fumble hooks and clean the Shakespeare reels.
What could we catch? I've been sitting in the pews
thinking about us a long time, long enough to see
a man can't live in jobless, friendless Cumberland
anymore. The soot owns even the fish.

I keep promising I'll come back, we'll get out,
you and me, like brothers, and I mean it.
A while ago a man with the look of a demented cousin
shuffled across this skittery floor and snatched up
the *Post-Gazette* and stuffed it in his coat
and nobody gave a damn because nobody cares

who comes or goes here or even who steals
what nobody wants: old news, photographs
of dead diesels behind chipped glass.

I'm the man who stole it and I wish you were here
to beat the hell out of me because what you said
a long time ago welts my face and won't go away.
I admit it isn't mine, even if it's nobody's.
Anyway, that's all I catch today – bad news.
I can't catch my nephew's life, my uncle's,
Big Daddy's, yours, or the ash-haired kids'
who fell down to sleep here after the war.

Outside new families pick their way along tracks
you and I have walked home on many nights.
Every face on the walls goes on smiling,
and, Grandfather, I wish I had the guts
to tell you this is a place I hope
I never have to go through again.

KEN SMITH

Zoo Station midnight

Drunks glitter in their liquids, fish
far down water where the light dies
on their armour of metal plates and crutches.

Outside in the city flowers of smashed glass,
the faithful in black spider armbands are back,
and the firestorm raging these forty years.

The animals wander the trapped streets,
furiously wounded. Here comes the midnight train
from Friedrichstrasse, from Warsaw, from Moscow.

It arrives in a flurry of flags and snow
with wolves howling, taking the width of the night
to get here. It arrives dragging the sheets

of its landscapes, – peasants, fires, shoes, no shoes,
speeches, snags of barbed wire, bayonets,
the apple blossoms of spring, the marsh air.

Late again he says, the stranger at my elbow,
bastards, sucking on a beer. In his black coat
and white hair he may be my double, my dark brother.

He knows a bar, a taxicab, a place to stay,
a woman, it takes a little paper money,
a word from him and we'll be out of here and into history.

[158]

JAMES THOMSON

In the Train

As we rush, as we rush in the Train,
   The trees and the houses go wheeling back.
But the starry heavens above the plain
   Come flying on our track.

All the beautiful stars of the sky,
   The silver doves of the forest of Night,
Over the dull earth swarm and fly,
   Companions of our flight.

We will rush ever on without fear;
   Let the goal be far, the flight be fleet!
For we carry the Heavens with us, dear,
   While the Earth slips from our feet!

KATRINA PORTEOUS

If My Train Will Come

If my train will come,
Quietly, in the night,
With no other sound than the slow
Creak of wheel upon wheel;
If, huge as a house but brighter,
Crouched at the edge of the fields
Like a steaming beast, it is waiting
Down the deserted road;
Though the colliery gate and the church
Where my mother and father were wed
Are all grown over at last
And the people I knew there dead now,
If a stranger alights
And, holding my breath, I see
That he has your eyes, your hair,
But does not remember me;
And if there follows a girl
With my face from years ago
And for miles by the sides of the tracks
The Durham grasses blow –
O, if my train will come
With its cargo of souls who have passed
Over this world to find me,
Will I go? Will I want to?

Ghost Train

Is it an illusion? It must be. Cesare
Pavese, sitting on a train, in a third-class
Carriage, alone with a woman who smokes.
He is too embarrassed to smile or make a pass
Among those empty seats that other women
Have at times vacated. It is history,
And the long train croaks
And shudders, smelling of upholstery,
Remaining empty, no place for encounters.

Public transport has been stitching together
The unfinished business of old Europe.
Believing in ghost buses that fail to stop
When requested, that appear only in foul weather,
Inhabitants of inner cities glamorise
Familiar places where the traffic chunters
Like some vigilant but dull
Official, an Argus with myopic eyes
Who cannot watch over his human cattle.
The ghost buses are empty, driverless.
They come upon one suddenly, with a noise
Of thunder and faint bells, their progress
Unsteady, vast overgrown toys
That have run away, and found this special route,
These special streets. Now someone tells a story
Of those who have managed the trick of boarding
By somehow leaping on, getting a foot

On the platform and grasping the ghost bar. According
To him their fate is terrible, a gory
Compound of brown wire, a cross between
A prison and a farmyard, shitty, poisonous.

Such buses and such trains keep rolling on.
Infected landscapes watch them, half asleep
And, perversely amorous,
They listen for flirtations in the spin
Of the wheel or the hiss of the smoke.
Now Cesare Pavese will not keep
Appointments, nor at this time of night
Is it possible to stay awake
And see the stations sweeping out of sight.

Train Song

Well I broke down in East St Louis
on the Kansas City line
and I drunk up all my money
that I borrowed every time
and I fell down at the derby
and now the night's black as a crow.
It was a train that took me away from here
but a train can't bring me home.
What made my dreams so hollow
was standing at the depot
with a steeple full of swallows
that could never ring the bell
and I come ten thousand miles away
with not one thing to show
well it was a train that took me away from here
but a train can't bring me home.
I remember when I left
without bothering to pack
you know I up and left with
just the clothes I had on my back
now I'm so sorry for what I've done
and I'm out here on my own
it was a train that took me away from here
but a train can't bring me home.

Charon

The conductor's hands were black with money;
Hold on to your ticket, he said, the inspector's
Mind is black with suspicion, and hold on to
That dissolving map. We moved through London,
We could see the pigeons through the glass but failed
To hear their rumours of wars, we could see
The lost dog barking but never knew
That his bark was as shrill as a cock crowing,
We just jogged on, at each request
Stop there was a crowd of aggressively vacant
Faces, we just jogged on, eternity
Gave itself airs in revolving lights
And then we came to the Thames and all
The bridges were down, the further shore
Was lost in fog, so we asked the conductor
What we should do. He said: Take the ferry
Faute de mieux. flicked the flashlight
And there was the ferryman just as Virgil
And Dante had seen him. He looked at us coldly
And his eyes were dead and his hands on the oar
Were black with obols and varicose veins
Marbled his calves and he said to us coldly:
If you want to die you will have to pay for it.

NORMAN NICHOLSON

Coastal Journey

A wet wind blows the waves across the sunset;
There is no more sea nor sky.
And the train halts where the railway line
Twists among the misty shifting sand,
Neither land nor estuary,
Neither wet nor dry.

In the blue dusk of the empty carriage
There is no more here nor there,
No more you nor me.
Green like a burning apple
The signal hangs in the pines beside the shore
And shines All Clear.

There is no more night nor evening;
No more now nor then.
There is only us and everywhere and always.
The train moves off again,
And the sandy pinetrees bend
Under the dark green berries of the rain.

ACKNOWLEDGEMENTS

The editors and publishers gratefully acknowledge permission to reprint
copyright material in this book as follows:

SIMON ARMITAGE: 'The Metaphor Now Standing at Platform 8' taken
from *Kid* © Simon Armitage and reproduced by permission of Faber
and Faber Ltd

JOHN BETJEMAN: 'Pershore Station, *or* a Liverish Journey First Class' and
'Thoughts in a Train' © John Betjeman, *Collected Poems* by permission
of John Murray

ALAN BROWNJOHN: 'The Train' © Alan Brownjohn (1983, 2006) by
permission of Enitharmon Press and Rosica Colin Ltd

CIARAN CARSON: 'Yes' © Ciaran Carson by permission of the poet and
The Gallery Press

WENDY COPE: 'Indeed 'tis true' © Wendy Cope from *Making Cocoa for
Kingsley Amis*. Reproduced by permission of Faber and Faber Ltd

FRANCES CORNFORD: 'To a Fat Lady Seen from a Train' from *Selected
Poems* © Frances Cornford. Reproduced by permission of Enitharmon
Press (1996)

WALTER DE LA MARE: 'The Railway Junctions' © the Literary Trustees of
Walter de la Mare & the Society of Authors

PETER DIDSBURY: 'The Guitar' © Peter Didsbury from *Scenes From A
Long Sleep: New and Collected Poems* by permission of Bloodaxe Books
(2003)

NORMAN DUBIE: 'The Train' © Norman Dubie. Reproduced by
permission of Copper Canyon Press

CAROL ANN DUFFY: 'The Way My Mother Speaks' from *The Other
Country* © Carol Ann Duffy 1990. Reproduced by permission of the
author c/o Rogers, Coleridge and White, London

HELEN DUNMORE: 'The Marshalling Yard' from *Out of the Blue: Poems
1975–2001* © Helen Dunmore. Reproduced by permission of Bloodaxe
Books 2001

DOUGLAS DUNN: 'Renfrewshire Traveller' © Douglas Dunn by permission
of United Agents and Faber and Faber Ltd

INDEX OF POETS

Abse, Dannie (b.1923) 70
Adcock, Fleur (b.1934) 132
Alexie, Sherman (b.1966) 94
Armitage, Simon (b.1963) 47
Ashbery, John (b.1927) 96
Auden, W. H. (1907–73) 49, 142

Barnes, William (1801–86) 5
Betjeman, John (1906–84) 51, 99
Bishop, Elizabeth (1911–79) 11
Brownjohn, Alan (b.1931) 41

Carson, Ciaran (b.1948) 131
Cope, Wendy (b.1945) 92
Cornford, Frances (1886–1960) 19, 53
Crawford, Robert (b.1959) 119

de la Mare, Walter (1873–1956) 45
Dickinson, Emily (1830–86) 4
Didsbury, Peter (b.1946) 24
Donaghy, Michael (1954–2004) 76
Dubie, Norman (b.1945) 33
Duffy, Carol Ann (b.1955) 133
Duhig, Ian (b.1954) 121
Dunmore, Helen (b.1952) 67
Dunn, Douglas (b.1942) 103
Durcan, Paul (b.1944) 105

Eliot, T. S. (1888–1965) 139

Fanthorpe, U. A. (1929–2009) 62
Farley, Paul (b.1965) 29
Flanders, Michael (1922–75) 38
Fuller, John (b.1937) 100

Glück, Louise (b.1943) 129
Gunn, Thom (1929–2004) 54

Hamilton, Ian (1938–2001) 63
Hardy, Thomas (1840–1928) 145
Harrison, Tony (b.1937) 64
Heaney, Seamus (b.1939) 3, 78, 81
Herbert, W. N. (b.1961) 82
Hofmann, Michael (b.1957) 65

Jarrell, Randall (1914–65) 21
Johnson, Robert (1911–38) 91

Koch, Kenneth (1925–2002) 12

Larkin, Philip (1922–85) 35, 69
Longley, Michael (b.1939) 127

MacCaig, Norman (1910–96) 128
McCarthy, Thomas (b.1954) 125
McGonagall, William
    (1825–1902) 146
McGuinness, Patrick (b.1968) 56
MacNeice, Louis (1907–63) 107, 130,
    164
Middleton, Christopher (b.1926) 57
Mitchell, Elma (1919–2000) 101
Montague, John (b.1929) 58
Morgan, Edwin (1920–2010) 83
Muldoon, Paul (b.1951) 150
Murray, Les (b.1938) 15, 109
Nicholson, Norman
    (1910–87) 165

O'Driscoll, Dennis (1954–2012) 59
Owen, Wilfred (1893–1918) 52

Pagis, Dan (1930–1986) 108
Parker, Junior (1932–1971) 151
Pastan, Linda (b.1932) 153
Phillips, Sam (1923–2003) 151
Porteous, Katrina (b.1960) 160
Porter, Peter (1929–2010) 111
Pound, Ezra (1885–1972) 75

Reznikoff, Charles (1894–1976) 85

Sandburg, Carl (1878–1967) 154
Simic, Charles (b.1938) 28
Simpson, Louis (1923–2012) 61
Smith, Dave (b.1942) 155
Smith, Ken (1938–2003) 158
Spender, Stephen (1909–95) 23
Sprackland, Jean (b.1962) 114
St Vincent Millay, Edna
  (1892–1950) 149
Stafford, William (1914–93) 20

Stevenson, Robert Louis
  (1850–94) 10
Stone, Ruth (1915–2011) 18, 118
Swann, Donald (1923–94) 38
Sweeney, Matthew (b.1951) 84
Szirtes, George (b.1948) 161
Szymborska, Wislawa
  (1923–2012) 71

Tartler, Grete (b.1948) 132
Thomas, Edward (1878–1917) 50
Thomson, James (1700–48) 159

Waits, Tom (b.1949) 163
Waldron, Mark (b.1960) 40
Whitman, Walt (1819–92) 8
Williams, Hugo (b.1942) 32, 93, 116
Williams, William Carlos
  (1883–1963) 6
Wordsworth, William
  (1770–1850) 42
Wright, James (1927–80) 31